The Complete Guide To Stay Anonymous In The Dark Net

Leonard Eddison

© **Copyright 2017 by Leonard Eddison**
All rights reserved.

This document is geared towards providing exact and reliable information with regards to the topic and issue covered. The publication is sold with the idea that the publisher is not required to render accounting, officially permitted, or otherwise, qualified services. If advice is necessary, legal or professional, a practiced individual in the profession should be ordered.

- From a Declaration of Principles which was accepted and approved equally by a Committee of the American Bar Association and a Committee of Publishers and Associations.

In no way is it legal to reproduce, duplicate, or transmit any part of this document in either electronic means or in printed format. Recording of this publication is strictly prohibited and any storage of this document is not allowed unless with written permission from the publisher. All rights reserved.

The information provided herein is stated to be truthful and consistent, in that any liability, in terms of inattention or otherwise, by any usage or abuse of any policies, processes, or directions contained within is the solitary and utter responsibility of the recipient reader. Under no circumstances will any legal responsibility or blame be held against the publisher for any reparation, damages, or monetary loss due to the information herein, either directly or indirectly.

Respective authors own all copyrights not held by the publisher.

The information herein is offered for informational purposes solely, and is universal as so. The presentation of the information is without contract or any type of guarantee assurance.

The trademarks that are used are without any consent, and the publication of the trademark is without permission or backing by the trademark owner. All trademarks and brands within this book are for clarifying purposes only and are the owned by the owners themselves, not affiliated with this document.

TABLE OF CONTENTS

TOR..0

INTRODUCTION TO TOR 7

CHAPTER 1 16

  IS TOR ILLEGAL? 5 FAST FACTS YOU NEED TO KNOW 16

CHAPTER 2 23

  WHAT IS TOR 23

CHAPTER 3 3131

  HOW TO USE TOR TO PROTECT YOUR PRIVACY 31

CHAPTER 4 466

  DOS AND DON'T OF TOR..............................466

CHAPTER 5 59

  SUMMARY(BEGINNERS GUIDE).........................589

BITCOIN 78

INTRODUCTION 81

CHAPTER 1 85
UNDERSTANDING BITCOIN 85
CHAPTER 2 93
THE TECHNICAL SIDE 93
CHAPTER 3 103
BITCOIN AS A CURRENCY 103
CHAPTER 4 119
WHAT HAS BITCOIN TAUGHT YS 119
CHAPTER 5 135
THE FUTURE OF BITCOIN ITSELF 135
CHAPTER 6 143
A FUTURE WITH BITCOIN 143
CONCLUSION 161

This page is intentionally left blank

INTRODUCTION TO TOR

When the U.S. Navy created Tor, a software that enables people to useInternet anonymously, it didn't envision someone like Edward Snowden.

Quite the opposite, military programmers originally built the software in the mid-1990s to support government spying operations.

Last montha photograph of Snowden, who leaked a trove of secrets about U.S. government surveillance, showed a sticker on his laptop supporting the Tor Project, the nonprofit that runs the anonymity network.

The image underscored the diverse andsometimesconflicting community of people using and supporting Tor in order to communicate anonymously on the Web.

Tor, which can be downloaded online, operates like a slower browser because it bounces packets of data across several continents to protect anonymity. Journalists, domestic abuse victims and dissidents living under repressive regimes use Tor to bypass government censors and to prevent their online movements from being tracked.

The U.S. State Department provides funding to the Tor Project to promote the freedom to use Internet in other countries. But the anonymizing software has alsobeen exploited by whistleblowers to leak sensitive U.S. government secrets. Though it's unclear whether Snowden used Tor to disclose details about NSA surveillance to reporters, Wikileaks has undoubtedly taken advantage of the software to protect whistleblowers.

"Tor's importance to Wikileaks cannot be understated",affirmed Julian Assange, theWikileaks founder, to Rolling Stone magazine in 2010.

While some people use Tor to traffic government secrets, criminals exploit Tor to peddle drugs, guns, murder-for-hire services, hacking tools and child pornography outside the reach of law enforcement, according to security experts.

Furthermore, to make sure that Tor is completely anonymous, it must protect all who are using it, even those whose actions are condemned by the U.S. government, as affirmed by Christopher Soghoian, the principal technologist at the American Civil Liberties Union, to The Huffington Post magazine. Soghaian also declared that, when you create a technology that allows people to communicate anonymously, you don't get to pick which activists use it. "If you want a network that's safe for dissidents and journalists, you have to allow the pedophiles, too," he added. "You have to take the good with the bad."

Tor masks people's online activities by routing traffic through layers of servers, or "nodes," around the world. Its creators likened the encryption method to layers of an onion, giving the software its original name: "The Onion Router."

About 500,000 people use Tor every day, according to the Tor Network, which consists of a global network of more than 3,000 volunteers who host servers and guarantee freedom of speech and online privacy.

Kelley Misata, a Tor Project spokeswoman, said that recent disclosures about NSA surveillance have raised the public's consciousness about anonymity tools. "With the recent news out there, people are becoming a bit more aware of prying eyes in their traffic," she affirmed.

The NSA revelations have also prompted Tor's supporters to disclose the network's limits in fighting government surveillance. "By itself, Tor does not protect the actual communications content once it leaves the Tor network," was written in a blog run by Tor Project a few months ago. The group said also that the software is "a key building block to build systems where it is no longer possible to go to a single party and obtain the full metadata, communications frequency, or contents."

Soghoian observesthat activity on Tor is unlikely to evade NSA surveillance: its multiple layers of encryption remain useful for people in order to evade government surveillance and censorship in Iran, Syria or China, but also for criminals who want to escape the watchful eye of law enforcement. "Just because the NSA can watch what's on the Tor network doesn't mean the sheriff in a small town can," he said.

In 2011, the FBI pointed out that an investigation into an illegal child pornography site was stymied because the site operators used the software to mask their location. "Because everyone (all Internet traffic) connected to the Tor network is anonymous, there is not currently a way to trace the origin of the website. As such, no other investigative leads exist", the FBI explained at the time.

Joseph V. DeMarco, the former head of the cyber crime unit at the U.S. attorney's office in New York, said that a criminal who uses Tor "means that avenue of investigation is blocked off".

In accordance with what DeMarco affirmed, the FBI has other investigative methods for tracking down cyber criminals, including search warrants and informants. But Tor makes it "extremely difficult, if not virtually impossible" for law enforcement to identify some illegal activities on the Internet. "Does that mean some people will get away with crimes? Sure", he said.

Some security experts have suggested that Tor's backers should be held responsible for supporting technology that thwarts criminal investigations.

"Ultimately, as with states, anonymization services should be held accountable for their users' behavior if they do not cooperate with law enforcement," Robert Knake, who is now director of cybersecurity for the White House, explained at a congressional committee in 2010.

But law enforcement also uses Tor to infiltrate illegal websites and catch criminals who use the software to hide from them, according to Soghoian.

In addition, Tor's creators, those in the government, say the more people using the network, the better. Tor's wide range of users, including those engaging in illegal activity, only further assist the software's original purpose: to cloak U.S. spying efforts, according to Michael Reed, one of Tor's original developers.

"Of course, we knew those would be other unavoidable uses for the technology," Reed wrote in an online forum in 2011, describing Tor's use by criminals, dissidents and those seeking porn. "But that was immaterial to the problem at hand we were trying to solve (and if those uses were going to give us more cover traffic to better hide what we wanted to use the network for, all the better...)"

For now, the Tor Project is focused on improving the software's image by attending conferences to educate law enforcement and dispel the notion that Tor is primarily a haven for criminal activity.

"We live in a world where if you use anonymizing tools, people assume it's for nefarious reasons," Misata, the Tor Project spokeswoman, said. "We're trying to put the word out that they can be used for very benign reasons. As more people use it, it will feel less scary."

And as more people use it, it becomes easier for Tor users to blend into the crowd and remain anonymous.

CHAPTER 1

IS TOR ILLEGAL? 5 FAST FACTS YOU NEED TO KNOW

As privacy awareness grows, the dark web has presented a more appealing and secure browsing alternative for some users compared to popular browsers.

The dark web is a network of websites that only run on anonymous browsers, which will hide the identity of the user and the people who run the sites. Perhaps the best-known anonymous browser is Tor, a platform that supports about 60,000 services like websites and chat services. It is legal to use Tor, but it does host illegal content.

In the popular imagination, anonymous browsers are a breeding ground for criminals. While the dark web does provide cover for illegal activities like storing child pornography or buying banned drugs, it also asserts a need for privacy that is often ignored on the larger Web.

Here's what you need to know about Tor:

1. It Protects the Identity of the User Through 'Hopping' Across Devices Worldwide

In order to protect your identity, Tor sends your communication through a random path in a network of relays until it reaches its destination. Tor will bounce your internet request across the network. This circuitous path will make it seem as if the request was coming from another device. While this process can make searching Tor agonizingly slow, it is the framework for anonymous browsing.

There are some limitations to anonymous browsing. While traffic within the Tor network is encrypted, it becomes visible when it retrieves information from the destination. Researchers have shown it's possible to eavesdrop on traffic from these exit nodes. This is why it is important to use encrypted connections like HTTPS, identified by the green lock and https:// in the address bar. Here are some other activities that may compromise your identity on Tor:

- Torrenting
- Using a Browser Plugin
- Downloading and opening a document while online
- Filling out web forms with personal information

Tor will encrypt your data within its network. Each computer node your message passes through will decrypt your data one layer at a time (hence the name 'onion router') to find out where to send the message next. Limiting access to information every step in the process has foiled most snooping attempts.

2. To Find a Site on Tor You Need to Know the Address of the Onion Service

Sites only available on the Tor network are known as Onion services. To help keep the services anonymous, the sites are only accessible through sixteen mostly random letters and numbers followed by ".onion", according to the Tor Browser User Manual. The list of Onion Services include marketplaces dedicated to making cryptocurrencies like Bitcoin untraceable and selling drugs.

3. Less Than Half of the Activity on the Dark Web is Illegal

Despite its nefarious undertones, much of the activity on the dark web is legal and even trivial. About 55 percent of content on the dark web is legal, according to Terbium Labs, a dark web data intelligence provider. Terbium Labs crawled 400 random sites one day in August for the study. So what kind of legal content lives on the dark web? Tor users can access websites like the dark-web replicas of popular sites like Facebook and ProPublica.

While some users seek the dark web as a sanctuary for illegal activities, others use it to safeguard their right to privacy. In fact, the public appetite for decentralized exchanges extends to cryptocurrencies like Bitcoin, as more people seek relief from the vice grip of surveillance nets. Here are some legitimate reasons people use Tor, according to the Tor Project.

Journalists who need to communicate with whistleblowers safely

NGO workers abroad who use Tor to connect to their home websites

The US Navy's intelligence gathering missions

Rape and abuse survivors who seek anonymous forums

4. The Dark Web Was Originally Meant to Safeguard Government Communications

"Onion Routing" was originally developed in order to protect intelligence communications online. The United States Naval Research Laboratory created Tor in the mid-1990s. The project was transferred to the Defense Advanced Research Projects Agency (DARPA) in 1997 and underwent its first round of software testing on 20 September 2002. Tor was publicly launched a year later.

Since the Naval Research Laboratory released Tor's code under a free license in 2004, privacy advocates have championed the software. The digital rights group Electronic Frontier Foundation funded Tor's continued development. Tor's developers founded the nonprofit The Tor Project to maintain Tor.

5. Anyone Can Volunteer to Be Part of Network Running Tor

Anyone can volunteer their computer to be part of the Dark Web network. As the number of volunteer relays grow, so does the network's speed. Tor relays can run on almost all operating systems, but works best for current distributions of Linux, according to the Tor Project. You can also contribute to the Tor community simply by downloading and using the service. As more people use the Dark Web, the level of anonymity increases, because it becomes harder to single out users.

CHAPTER 2

WHAT IS TOR

Tor (originally called The Onion Router because it layers your traffic like an onion) is a free network of servers, or 'nodes', that randomly route internet traffic between each other in order to obfuscate the origin of the data. The Tor Browser can significantly increase a user's privacy and anonymity online. In internal documents, the NSA even refers to Tor as "the king of high-secure, low latency internet anonymity."

Tor is short for "The Onion Router".

Tor is often viewed negatively by the press and law enforcement agencies, but it has many positive benefits. Journalists and their sources rely on it to communicate securely and anonymously, without fear of government interference. Secure communication is essential in whistleblowing cases, like the Edward Snowden revelations. Similarly, Tor is important for law enforcement as it allows for covert operations and investigations online. Tor currently has about two million daily users worldwide, most of them originating from the United States, Germany, and Russia.

You can use Tor to hide your IP address, browse the dark web, and run a server anonymously.

Tor does not replace your VPN, as it only anonymizes your browsing and a few other select services (which need to be specifically configured).

Connecting to Tor through VPN connection is a great way to maintain your internet privacy and security. Not only will it hide your browsing data from your VPN company, it will also hide your home IP address from the Tor entry node.

How Tor really works

Let's pretend that computers and the internet don't exist and people still communicate with what we now call "traditional mail".

In this horrifying alternate world, people actually still read books. But how could you buy one when you can't be bothered to leave the house? You could use the yellow pages to look up the address of a publishing house, then send them a postcard.

On that card, you could express a desire to obtain a book you like, and you could include your own address so that the publisher knows where to send it to.

The problem is that everyone along the delivery route can see what everyone wants to read. They can make copies of everything or simply keep lists of who requested what.

Envelopes protect the content

A simple level of protection would be to put requests into sealed envelopes. Seals are impossible to open without breaking them, so all the post office could do is maintain lists of what gets delivered where, without knowing the contents of the envelopes.

This information—pertaining to, for example, the size and weight of the envelope, and the identities of the sender and recipient—is called the metadata.

Metadata reveals a lot. For example, you can tell if you've received a speeding ticket just from looking at the envelope. And so can the mailman.

This is very close to how the internet works today. Cryptographic seals go one step further by being impossible to open. Unfortunately basic encryption, like Transport Layer Security (TLS), is not yet standard across the web. (You can tell when this is active, as a green lock will appear in your address bar).

Tor circuits rely on a system of nodes

To send requests anonymously in the Tor network, you start by establishing a Tor circuit. To do this, you send your "sealed postcard" to a random Tor node. This could be a residential or commercial address. It could be your neighbor's house, or it could be a big building in a faraway country. This is your entry node, and all your sealed mail will be sent to this address. All the mail that you receive will also come from this address.

Your entry node will forward your mail to yet another node, which will again forward it on to another node, the exit node. Only the exit node knows the address of your intended recipient.

The following is an explanation of how the system of nodes works:

The entry node can see who you are, but not what you request or who you request it from.

The middle node cannot see anything. It is important because it separates the exit and entry nodes from each other.

The exit node can only see what you request, but not who you are. Ideally you will be using TLS to make your request, so the exit node can see who you are requesting something from, but not the content of your request.

Tor is run by volunteers

A system like Tor could at least hypothetically work with physical mail, but the effort needed to reroute mail and seal envelopes would be gigantic. The Tor system is far easier to accomplish electronically, but the network still relies on volunteers who run Tor nodes on their servers or at home.

The exit node is the most fragile spot in this chain. If the connection to the website you are visiting is not using TLS encryption, there is no guarantee that the exit node is not logging the contents of your requests, altering them, or injecting malware into them. If your system is not correctly configured, things like cookies, or the contents of your communications, could still identify you.

Use .Onion addresses to avoid exit nodes

There is a way to entirely avoid using exit nodes. But for that to work, the website you are visiting needs to be set up with a .onion address. This address is not like a regular domain name, because there is no way to formally register it. The domains are usually alphanumeric strings generated from a public cryptographic key. Using such a domain not only removes the exit node from the equation, it also makes it impossible for both the user and the site to know where the other party is.

Facebook and Blockchain.info are also among the small number of sites that have TLS certificates issued for their .onion sites. This does not make the content significantly more private or secure, but can help to identify whether the site you are connected to really is the site you wanted to reach. Many sites are exclusively reachable through their .onion address, in an attempt to remain uncensorable and to keep their location a secret. This part of the Internet is usually called the dark web.

CHAPTER 3

HOW TO USE TOR TO PROTECT YOUR PRIVACY

Connect to the Dark Web with the Tor browser

The most common way for you to access the dark web or use the Tor network is through the Tor Browser. The browser looks and feels like Firefox, but comes optimized for security and privacy. It has the NoScript and HTTPS Everywhere extensions pre-installed to protect you from malicious Flash or Javascript exploits. It also makes sure cookies are deleted at startup and websites don't have access to any information that can be used to identify you.

The Tor Browser is easy to run. In fact, it doesn't require any installation at all and you can just run the .exc or .dmg files direct from your USB stick. This makes it possible to bring the browser into an environment where you cannot install software, such as your school or office.

After starting the browser, it will ask you about your network. If your network is clear from censorship you can start surfing the internet immediately. Otherwise, you will be asked to give more information, such as your local proxy service, which will help the browser circumvent the censorship.

You can navigate websites in the same way you are used to. Additionally, you can resolve addresses on the dark web. These are addresses ending in .onion where the server cannot easily be identified, censored or seized. The online publication ProPublica (http://propub3r6espa33w.onion/) and Facebook (https://facebookcorewwwi.onion) both operate such servers, for example.

The Tor Browser makes it easy to be secure and private, but we still need to make sure not to voluntarily hand over information that could compromise us.

Practice safe browsing habits

The Tor Browser will not do everything your regular browser can do, but that's for good reason. Don't be tempted to install plug-ins or add-ons, because they might connect back to servers outside of the Tor network, revealing your IP address and other information about your browsing history.

In the Tor Browser, you need to make more sure than usual that you are connecting to websites using HTTPS. Just like on public Wi-Fi, there is no way to know who is running the exit node, or whether it is secure. There is also no way of telling what the node is doing. It could be reading, intercepting, or even altering your information. The exit node might even try to strip Transport Layer Security (TLS) from the site entirely, so always check if the lock in the address bar is visible! Otherwise, a malicious exit node might establish an encrypted connection between itself and the server you are connecting to, meaning the exit node can read the traffic between you and your server.

While the Tor Browser deletes your cookies and history upon each startup, surfing the web could trigger compromising cookies to be loaded on your machine. For example, logging into Facebook in one tab will set cookies that can identify you to other pages as a specific Facebook user.

Also be aware of any content you download. Even PDFs and Word documents might contain little snippets of code that could reveal your personal Internet protocol (IP) address. The safest thing to do is to open such documents on a virtual machine, or when your computer is offline.

The Tor network protects your metadata by hiding it among all the other traffic. If your load on the Tor network is very high (i.e. you operate a very popular dark web site), you might be identifiable due to your heavy traffic.

Set up Tor as a proxy

Browsing is not the only thing you can do with Tor. It can also be set up as a proxy service, so that any data you point to gets routed through the network.

Many applications support the SOCKS5 proxy that Tor uses. Pidgin, Adium, Dropbox, and Bitcoin wallets like Core and Electrum all allow you to route your traffic through the Tor network so you can stay anonymous. For a truly anonymous solution, though, you need to make sure to sign up for all your accounts while connected to Tor, download all the software through Tor, and never connect to these services through the regular internet.

You can also use Tor the other way (a reverse proxy), i.e., make the services on your web server available through a .onion address, for example. This protects both you and your users from bad exit nodes and unwanted server location reveals.

It's not recommended to torrent through the Tor network. Modern bittorrent clients use UDP as a protocol, which does not work over Tor. As a result, your data will either not be transmitted at all or transmitted outside of Tor, revealing your IP address in the process.

Connect to Tor via bridges and VPN when Tor is blocked

Many networks ban any kind of Tor traffic through their systems by blacklisting all known entry nodes. To get around this ban, you can connect to a bridge. A bridge functions similarly to an entry node, except that you have to obtain IP addresses manually. Using a bridge to connect to the Tor network does not have any significant drawbacks, but in many situations will not be able to circumvent Tor obstructions. For better results, first connect to your VPN, then to the Tor network.

When you are connected with a VPN, neither the sites you are visiting nor the Tor entry nodes will know your true location, though the VPN company will. However, the VPN company cannot see the content of your traffic, even if they tried to, as the traffic is encrypted between you and the Tor entry node.

Theoretically, there is also the option of connecting first to the Tor network, then tunneling a VPN through it. This makes it impossible for your VPN provider to know where you are, and ensures exit nodes can't read or alter your traffic. Unfortunately most VPN providers do not support this function.

Depending on whether you use Tor, VPN, or a combination of the two, sites and networks can see different information about you.

How to securely share files using Tor

While you shouldn't (and often can't) use the Tor network to hide your torrent traffic, the Tor network provides you with one of the most convenient ways to share files with other people. It's called OnionShare and was developed by Micah Lee. It is very secure, and much more convenient than sending email attachments and or using Dropbox.

With Onionshare, you just select the file on your computer and a link to it is generated. You can then share this link with the intended recipient, via any application. You and the recipient will need to keep the Tor browser open during the entire process. Sharing files using Tor ensures that the sender and recipient never know each other's locations.

Onionshare is the one truly anonymous file sharing method. Take note, however, that anyone with the link will be able to download the file, so you should share the link in an encrypted fashion, for example with OTR (Off-The-Record).

There is also a neat option that allows you to close the server after the item has been downloaded. That way you can be absolutely certain that the item is only accessed once. If your contact received it, you can be sure no one else did.

Coming soon: Private messaging with Tor Messenger

The Tor Messenger is still in beta and doesn't yet promise full security. It is built on Mozilla's Instantbird and serves solely as a client for your existing chat accounts, such as Jabber, Twitter, IRC, and Yahoo.

Tor Messenger includes OTR encryption protocol and will reliably hide the contents of your messages from even the most advanced hackers. It is preconfigured to route all your traffic through the Tor network, hiding your location from the server. Be cautious, though, as the server can still collect metadata, and could possibly be used to attempt man-in-the-middle attacks.

Safe tools for whistleblowers

SecureDrop (originally called DeadDrop) is software that makes it easier to safely leak information to the press over the Tor network. It was originally developed by Aaron Swartz and is currently being maintained by the Freedom of the Press Foundation. It has been adopted by ProPublica, The Intercept, and The Guardian, amongst others.

SecureDrop runs on a server belonging to a journalist or news organization that is only reachable via Tor. The whistleblower can upload any kind of document to this server, for which they receive a code. This unique code can later be used to submit more information, or communicate securely and anonymously with the journalists.

Tor for Android

Orbot, the Tor browser for Android, can be found in the Google Play store and the Guardian Project official app repository. You can also use Orbot as a proxy to configure other apps, such as Chat Secure, to route traffic through the Tor network. This combination gives you similar protections as using the Tor messenger on desktop.

Tor for iOS

Tor is not officially available on iOS devices, although system-wide Tor apps might now become possible with new features introduced in iOS 9.

Tor for Tails

The Amnesic Incognito Live System is an operating system based on Linux that you can run from a DVD or USB stick. It comes pre-installed with the most important encryption software, like Pretty Good Privacy (PGP) and OTR. It will route all your traffic through the Tor network by default. This makes it far easier to remain truly anonymous, and it also mitigates threats of bugs or attacks.

You can easily carry it with you and it does not need to be installed on the computer you are running. The Amnesic Incognito Live System lets you safely and easily maintain a separate identity on your own computer or a public device.

Even with Tor, you are still at risk

While the Tor network is generally considered secure, it should not be overestimated in regards of what it does. Applications like the Tor Browser and Tor Messenger come pre-configured to route your traffic through the Tor network and minimize your risk of leaking personal information, but there are still many ways in which your identity might be compromised by a malicious third-party entity.

In the past, attacks have lured users to compromised websites where a javascript exploit bypasses the Tor network and reveals the user's IP address.

If an attacker is able to gain control of a large portion of the network, they could perform network analysis to correlate traffic on the entry nodes with traffic on the exit nodes. The attacker could then work out who is viewing what content.

This is especially risky for operators of big and popular sites on the dark web who want to keep their location anonymous. The more traffic they attract, the easier it is for an adversary to figure out where their traffic is going.

How to contribute to Tor

While the Tor network is still primarily funded by the United States government, it relies on the efforts of activists and volunteers to stay secure. Additional resources to the project will make it more balanced and less dependent on government and military support. You can help out by doing any of the following.

Use Tor. You will get internet privacy yourself, and also help to establish the network as an important tool for everyday users.

Become a Tor developer. It is worth major street cred to build on top of the leading anonymity network! You can help bring in whatever skill you have to increase the Tor Project's security, documentation, and features.

Donate to the Tor project. The Tor project accepts Paypal, Dwolla, and Bitcoins. There is still so much to be done!

Donate to a node provider. If a relay doesn't have a Bitcoin address entered in its contact field, you can donate directly with this tool.

Run a relay. If you have extra bandwidth available, you can run a relay from home or your own server.

CHAPTER 4

DOS AND DON'T OF TOR

Don't use Windows. Just don't. This also means don't use the Tor Browser Bundle on Windows. Vulnerabilities in the software in TBB figure prominently in both the NSA slides and FBI's recent takedown of Freedom Hosting.

If you can't construct your own workstation capable of running Linux and carefully configured to run the latest available versions of Tor, a proxy such as Privoxy, and a web browser (with all outgoing clearnet access firewalled), consider using Tails or Whonix instead, where most of this work is done for you. It's absolutely critical that outgoing access be firewalled so that third party applications cannot accidentally leak data about your location.

If you are using persistent storage of any kind, ensure that it is encrypted. Current versions of LUKS are reasonably safe, and major Linux distributions will offer to set it up for you during their installation. TrueCrypt might be safe, though it's not nearly as well integrated into the OS. BitLocker might be safe as well, though you still shouldn't be running Windows. Even if you are in a country where rubber hosing is legal, such as the UK, encrypting your data protects you from a variety of other threats.

Remember that your computer must be kept up to date. Whether you use Tails or build your own workstation from scratch or with Whonix, update frequently to ensure you are protected from the latest security vulnerabilities. Ideally you should update each time you begin a session, or at least daily. Tails will notify you at startup if an update is available.

Be very reluctant to compromise on JavaScript, Flash and Java. Disable them all by default. If a site requires any of these, visit somewhere else. Enable scripting only as a last resort, only temporarily, and only to the minimum extent necessary to gain functionality of a web site that you have no alternative for.

Viciously drop cookies and local data that sites send you. Neither TBB nor Tails do this well enough for my tastes; consider using an addon such as Self-Destructing Cookies to keep your cookies to a minimum. Of zero.

Your workstation must be a laptop; it must be portable enough to be carried with you and quickly disposed of or destroyed.

Don't use Google to search the internet. A good alternative is Startpage; this is the default search engine for TBB, Tails, and Whonix. Plus it won't call you malicious or ask you to fill out CAPTCHAs.

Your Environment

Tor contains weaknesses which can only be mitigated through actions in the physical world. An attacker who can view both your local Internet connection, and the connection of the site you are visiting, can use statistical analysis to correlate them.

Never use Tor from home, or near home. Never work on anything sensitive enough to require Tor from home, even if you remain offline. Computers have a funny habit of liking to be connected. This also applies to anywhere you are staying temporarily, such as a hotel. Never performing these activities at home helps to ensure that they cannot be tied to those locations. (Note that this applies to people facing advanced persistent threats. Running Tor from home is reasonable and useful for others, especially people who aren't doing anything themselves but wish to help by running an exit node, relay, or bridge.

Limit the amount of time you spend using Tor at any single location. While these correlation attacks do take some time, they can in theory be completed in as little as a day. And while the jackboots are very unlikely to show up the same day you fire up Tor at Starbucks, they might show up the next day. I recommend for the truly concerned to never use Tor more than 24 hours at any single physical location; after that, consider it burned and go elsewhere. This will help you even if the jackboots show up six months later; it's much easier to remember a regular customer than someone who showed up one day and never came back. This does mean you will have to travel farther afield, especially if you don't live in a large city, but it will help to preserve your ability to travel freely.

When you go out to perform these activities, leave your cell phone turned on and at home.

Your Mindset

Many Tor users get caught because they made a mistake, such as posting their real email address in association with their activities. You must avoid this as much as possible, and the only way to do so is with careful mental discipline.

Think of your Tor activity as pseudonymous, and create in your mind a virtual identity to correspond with the activity. This virtual person does not know you and will never meet you, and wouldn't even like you if he knew you. He must be kept strictly mentally separated.

If you must use public internet services, create completely new accounts for this pseudonym. Never mix them; for instance do not browse Facebook with your real email address after having used Twitter with your pseudonym's email on the same computer. Wait until you get home.

By the same token, never perform actions related to your pseudonymous activity via the clearnet, unless you have no other choice (e.g. to sign up for a provider who blocks Tor), and take extra precautions regarding your location when doing so.

If you need to make and receive phone calls, purchase an anonymous prepaid phone for the purpose. This is difficult in some countries, but it can be done if you are creative enough. Pay cash; never use a debit or credit card to buy the phone or top-ups. Never insert its battery or turn it on if you are within 10 miles (16 km) of your home, nor use a phone from which the battery cannot be removed. Never place a

SIM card previously used in one phone into another phone. Never give its number or even admit its existence to anyone who knows you by your real identity. This may need to include your family members.

Hidden Services

These are big in the news lately, with the recent takedown of at least two high-profile hidden services, Silk Road and Freedom Hosting. The bad news is, hidden services are much weaker than they could or should be. The good news is, the NSA doesn't seem to have done much with them (though the NSA slides mention a GCHQ program named ONIONBREATH which focuses on hidden services, nothing else is yet known about it).

In addition, since hidden services must often run under someone else's physical control, they are vulnerable to being compromised via that other party. Thus it's even more important to protect the anonymity of the service, as once it is compromised in this manner, it's pretty much game over.

The advice given above is sufficient if you are merely visiting a hidden service. If you need to run a hidden service, do all of the above, and in addition do the following. Note that these tasks require an experienced system administrator; performing them without the relevant experience will be difficult or impossible.

Do not run a hidden service in a virtual machine unless you also control the physical host. Designs in which Tor and a service run in firewalled virtual machines on a firewalled physical host are OK, provided it is the physical host which you are in control of, and you are not merely leasing cloud space.

A better design for a Tor hidden service consists of two physical hosts, leased from two different providers though they may be in the same datacenter.

On the first physical host, a single virtual machine runs with Tor. Both the host and VM are firewalled to prevent outgoing traffic other than Tor traffic and traffic to the second physical host. The second physical host will then contain a VM with the actual hidden service. Again, these will be firewalled in both directions. The connection between them should be secured with IPSec, OpenVPN, etc. If it is suspected that the host running Tor may be compromised, the service on the second server may be immediately moved (by copying the virtual machine image) and both servers decommissioned. Both of these designs can be implemented fairly easily with Whonix.

Hosts leased from third parties are convenient but especially vulnerable to attacks where the service provider takes a copy of the hard drives. If the server is virtual, or it is physical but uses RAID storage, this can be done without taking the server offline. Again, do not lease cloud space, and carefully monitor the hardware of the physical host. If the RAID array shows as degraded, or if the server is inexplicably down for more than a few moments, the server should be considered compromised, since there is no way to distinguish between a simple hardware failure and a compromise of this nature.

Ensure that your hosting provider offers 24x7 access to a remote console (in the hosting industry this is often called a KVM though it's usually implemented via IPMI which can also install the operating system. Use temporary passwords/passphrases during the installation, and change them all after you have Tor up and running (see below). The remote console also allows you to run a fully encrypted physical host, reducing the risk of data loss through physical compromise; however, in this case the passphrase must be changed every time the system is booted (even this does not mitigate all possible attacks, but it does buy you time).

Your initial setup of the hosts which will run the service must be over clearnet, albeit via ssh; however, to reiterate, they must not be done from home or from a location you have ever visited before. As we have seen, it is not sufficient to simply use a VPN. This may cause you issues with actually signing up for the service due to fraud protection that such providers may use. How to deal with this is outside the scope of this answer, though.

Once you have Tor up and running, never connect to any of the servers or virtual machines via clearnet again. Configure hidden services which connect via ssh to each host and each of the virtual machines, and always use them. If you must connect via clearnet to resolve a problem, again, do so from a location you will never visit again.

Hidden services must be moved regularly, even if compromise is not suspected. A 2013 paper described an attack which can locate a hidden service in just a few months for around $10,000 in cloud compute charges, which is well within the budget of even some individuals. It is safer, though not at all convenient, to move the hidden service at least monthly. Ideally it should be moved as frequently as possible, though this quickly veers into the impractical. Note that it will take approximately an hour for the Tor network to recognize the new location of a moved hidden service.

Anonymity is hard. Technology alone, no matter how good it is, will never be enough. It requires a clear mind and careful attention to detail, as well as real-world actions to mitigate weaknesses that cannot be addressed through technology alone. As has been so frequently mentioned, the attackers can be bumbling fools who only have sheer luck to rely on, but you only have to make one mistake to be ruined. We call them "advanced persistent threats" because, in part, they are persistent. They won't give up, and you must not.

CHAPTER 5

SUMMARY (BEGINNERS GUIDE)

What is Tor?

When you connect to the internet you're assigned an IP address by your service provider. This IP is easily traceable to your name and physical location, and it's directly tied with your unencrypted web browsing activity, as well. ISPs can monitor, log, and even sell this data to third parties without your consent. That's where Tor comes into play.

Tor is a network built around anonymity. It's managed by The Tor Project and has been operational since 2002, though precursors to Tor can be traced back even further. Tor works by using onion routing to encapsulate data in layers of encryption and passing that data through a series of nodes. Each node peels away one layer of encryption, revealing the next layer along with instructions on where the data goes next. By the time the final layer is decrypted, the data will reach its location, leaving almost no trace behind.

Using the Tor network is a bit like passing a note across a crowded room of people, each of whom has their eyes closed. You pass it to someone at random, that person passes it to another person, and so on. When it reaches the other side of the room, nobody knows who the note originated from, nor can they tell which person handed it to them. The Tor network protects your identity by encrypting your traffic and making everything you do as anonymous as possible.

Tor and the Tor Browser

The Tor network is used by a number of different software suites, the most well-known of which is the Tor Browser. The Tor Browser works like any other browser, only instead of sending information directly to and from your computer, it leverages the Tor network to provide a strong measure of privacy and anonymity.

The Tor Browser is basically a highly customized version of Firefox. This gives it the ability to access any part of the web, just like a regular browser. However, due to its security conscious design, the Tor Browser disables a number of common web technologies such as Adobe Flash and JavaScript, rendering many websites unusable.

The Tor Browser is an open source project with versions available for Windows, Mac, and Linux computers as well as smartphone and tablet releases for devices running Android. Third parties have created unofficial versions of the browser that also use the Tor network, giving iPhone and iPad owners the ability to sure safely, as well.

Installing the Tor Browser

Using the Tor Browser is the most direct way of leveraging the privacy power of the Tor network. It's simple, it's direct, it's free, and it's easy to get started. There are several ways to download and install the browser, including portable versions, unstable versions, and compiling directly from the source. Most people who use the Tor Browser get it through the Tor Browser Bundle. This is by far the easiest way to access the Tor network, as everything you need is packaged into a single download you can run and install with just a few clicks.

Install on Windows

Visit the Tor Browser Bundle download page in your web browser.

Click the purple "Download" button. You may need to change operating system options to get the right version.

When the file downloads, run the installer.

Launch the Tor browser when the installation completes.

Click "Connect" to access the Tor network.

Click the onion icon just to the left of the URL bar.

Choose "Security settings"

Move the slider all the way up to "High" for maximum privacy.

Surf the web through the Tor Browser.

Install on MacOS

Visit the Tor Browser Bundle download page in your web browser.

Click the purple "Download" button. You may need to change operating system options to get the right version.

Save the file on your computer.

Click to open the .dmg file.

Drag the included file into your Applications folder.

Pin the Tor Browser on your dock and launch it.

Click "Connect" to access the Tor network.

Click the onion icon just to the left of the URL bar.

Choose "Security settings"

Move the slider all the way up to "High" for maximum privacy.

Surf the web through the Tor Browser.

Install on Linux

Visit the Tor Browser Bundle download page in your web browser.

Click the purple "Download" button. You may need to change operating system options to get the right version.

Save the file to a local directory.

Open a terminal and type the following command: tar -xvJf tor-browser-linux32-6.5.2_LANG.tar.xz

In the line above, replace the 32 with a 64 if you downloaded the 64-bit version, and switch LANG with the language you downloaded. You might need to adjust the version numbers if the file notes something different, as well.

Switch to the Tor Browser directory in the terminal, replacing LANG with your language code: cd tor-browser_LANG

Run the Tor Browser.

The Tor Launcher will appear on your screen. Connect through this and the browser will open.

Surf the web through the Tor Browser.

Install on Android

There's an official Tor Browser for Android called Orfox. To let it use the Tor network, however, you'll need to install another program first. Both are open source and available through Google Play.

First, install Orbot from Google Play.

Run Orbot and let it stay active in the background.

Install Orfox, the Tor Browser for Android, from Google Play.

Launch Orfox and use it to surf the web with enhanced Tor network security.

Install on iOS

The Tor Project doesn't maintain an official Tor Browser for iPhone, iPad, or other iOS devices. There is a free and open source Onion Browser created by Mike Tigas that leverages the Tor network performs most of the same functions.

Visit the Onion Browser download page on the iTunes App Store.

Install the app on your iPhone or iPad.

Surf the web through the Onion Browser.

Change Your Habits for Better Privacy

It's a common misconception that installing and using the Tor Browser is a bulletproof solution for all online dangers. Using the Tor network does have a wide range of advantages, but it's far from a quick data privacy cure-all. You'll need to change some of your normal web browsing habits to ensure you remain anonymous. This involves disabling certain plug-ins, keeping an eye on cloud storage programs, and being smart about which websites you log into.

Follow these tips to ensure a higher level of privacy online:

Use HTTPS versions of websites – You're probably familiar with the "http" letters used at the beginning of websites. That extra "s" denotes secured versions of those sites and means they encrypt the data that goes to and from their servers. Most shopping, e-mail, and banking services use HTTPS by default. The data passed to and from a Tor exit node to the intended website is unencrypted, making it an extremely weak part of the process. If you connect to a secure HTTPS site, you're a lot safer. The Tor Browser Bundle includes the HTTPS Everywhere extension, which forces secure connections with major websites whenever possible.

Don't use plug-ins or add-ons – The Tor Browser is based on Firefox, which means it's possible to use a handful of Firefox add-ons just like an ordinary browser. The Tor Browser Bundle even comes with a few security-minded add-ons pre-installed, such as HTTPS Everywhere and NoScript, all of which are safe to use and enhance your anonymity. To stay as secure as possible, you should leave the plug-ins list at that. Adding new plug-ins could put your privacy at risk, both by directly circumventing Tor protection and by encouraging you to relax your habits while using the Tor Browser.

Disable JavaScript, Flash, ActiveX, Java, and QuickTime – Technologies like these power a great deal of the web's interactive content. They can also compromise your privacy by sharing information about your system and location with websites, even if you're using the Tor network. The Tor Browser disables all of these on its high and medium security settings.

Don't use torrents over Tor – Many file sharing and torrent applications are known to ignore proxy settings and connect directly to trackers even when instructed otherwise. If you configure your torrent software to use the Tor network, it simply might not do it. [In case you want to use it, we have found the best VPNs for torrenting, the ones that actually take your privacy serious]

Don't log into anything through Tor – One of the first things people do when getting on the internet is to log in and check their e-mail. While this is certainly possible through the Tor Browser, it kind of defeats the purpose of the entire network, as you're still sharing data with outside sources. For the ultimate in privacy, don't log into any website or provide details of any account while using Tor.

Don't open files downloaded through Tor – This is a commonly ignored piece of advice that can completely destroy your online privacy. Most users browsing through Tor are interested in accessing sensitive information. If they download a file through the Tor Browser and open it, that file could access the internet without passing through the Tor network, thus sharing your real IP and location. It's best to disconnect from the internet before opening any downloaded content.

Use Tails OS – The Tails OS was designed to use the Tor network. Everything that passes through the operating system is encrypted and anonymized, and there's no trace of data left behind. Tails even runs from a DVD, SD card, or USB stick with no installation required. With Tails and the Tor Browser both in use, your online activities are much more secure. See the section below for more information on how to install and use Tails OS.

Using Tor with the Tails Operating System

Tails is a lightweight live operating system designed to keep private data private safe and leave no trace of information on the device it's running on. It uses state-of-the-art cryptographic tools to protect your data and allow you to circumvent censorship almost anywhere you go. Better still, Tails runs on almost any computer simply by inserting a DVD, USB stick, or SD card.

Tails uses the Tor network by default, encrypting and anonymizing every piece of information that leaves your computer. It also comes with the Tor Browser and a secure instant messaging service to make all of your online activities as private and anonymous as possible.

To use the Tails operating system you'll need two USB sticks and a separate internet device to read instructions while the installation takes place. The website below walks you through the process step by step.

Use your web browser to download Tails OS.
Run the Tails installer and follow the on screen instructions.
Restart your computer and boot directly into Tails OS.

Enter your Wi-Fi or connection details to access the internet.

Open Tor (included with the Tails download) and browse the web at your leisure.

Tor and the Dark Web

Tor and the dark web have a long history together. Using the Tor network is the only way you can access .onion links, which is where most of the deep web's content is hidden. The Tor Browser also provides a bit of security for anyone exploring the hidden depths of the dark web. The two are closely linked, but it's important to realize that all Tor users aren't necessarily using the browser or the network to access illicit content. Privacy is still Tor's number one focus.

If you intend on using the Tor Browser to access the dark web, you'll need to take every precaution to preserve your privacy. Read our full guide on How to Access the Dark Web and Deep Web for more information.

Can You Use Tor for Everyday Browsing?

While it's possible to use Tor or the Tor browser for everyday tasks on the internet, most users find it's an exercise in frustration. With all of the encryption and re-routing that's going on, Tor tends to be extremely slow, sometimes as much as 70% slower than your home internet. This leads to endless waits for pages to load and drops download speeds to practically nothing. On top of that, because Tor disables so many modern web technologies that are inherently unsafe, you'll find many common websites such as YouTube are completely inaccessible.

The Tor Browser is a great tool for accessing certain websites, especially geo-restricted content, censored websites, and content sealed up on the dark web through onion links. When you're traveling it's not a bad idea to use Tor for basic tasks, either, and it does wonders for anyone who lives in an area where certain websites are blocked or restricted. It's also great for journalists who need to preserve their anonymity while researching and passing information to other sources. You'll need a lot of patience if you use it for all of your daily internet tasks, however.

Isn't Using a Regular Browser's Incognito Mode Safe Enough?

Private tabs on browsers like Chrome, Firefox, Opera, and Safari were made for one purpose: hiding online activity from your local computer. In essence, all they do is make sure everything you access in a private tab doesn't leave a trail in your local browsing history. Incognito mode doesn't prevent ISPs from tracking you, nor will it protect your privacy once data leaves your computer.

Tor versus Proxies

Using a proxy to hide your location sounds like a similar solution as using the Tor network. They both help bypass censorship laws, they both make users anonymous, and both protect a user's location and online activities. The difference lies in how each of these services provide anonymity.

With a proxy your traffic is directed through a non-local server, assigning you a different IP address so activity can't be linked to your computer. The downside of using a proxy is that it creates a single point of failure. The proxy provider knows who you are, especially if you pay to use the service. This means they can unlock your encrypted data and use it for their own purposes, all without your knowledge. Using a proxy can be dangerous if privacy is important to you, especially if it's a low quality or free proxy.

Tor neatly circumvents the limitations of a proxy by distributing its anonymizing services over thousands of computers. Instead of sending your traffic through one non-local server, it's sent through at least three, completely at random, and all encrypted. It's difficult, if not impossible, to track the path data travels through the Tor network.

Using Tor with a VPN

Using Tor alone isn't enough to protect your online browsing habits. Even with the encryption and anonymity provided by the network, it's still possible to monitor someone's traffic, analyze it, and find its source. While measures such as these are usually reserved for high value targets, there are still a number of reasons you should pair Tor with a virtual private network.

Somewhat similar to Tor, VPNs encrypt your internet traffic and allow it to pass through your local ISP anonymously. Information is sent to a server of your choosing, then it gets decrypted and utilized back on your own device. The privacy offered by a VPN is more focused on preventing data leaks, not obscuring your identity, but there's some overlap between the two.

There are two ways to use Tor with a VPN. Both carry some drawbacks and benefits, but both also provide extra privacy over using one or the other.

Method 1: VPN to the Tor Network – The simplest way to use a VPN with Tor is to sign up for a VPN service, download the Tor Browser, then have both of them running at the same time. This method sends data through your VPN first, then through the Tor network for an extra measure of anonymity. It's also extremely easy to do. The downside is that the typical Tor exit node vulnerability still applies, meaning your data could theoretically be tracked if someone was determined enough to do so.

Method 2: Tor Network to a VPN – This is the commonly suggested method of combining Tor with a VPN. Data goes from your computer, through the

Tor network where it's encrypted and anonymized, then through your VPN. This reduces the risks of a VPN logging your information, as data the VPN receives will already be anonymized through the Tor network. The set-up is a bit more convoluted, however, as you'll need to use a security-oriented operating system such as Whonix to make sure data follows the correct path.

As it is possible to buy products and services in the deep web only by using Bitcoins, the next book will give you a good insight of how bitcoins works.

Bitcoin

A Deep Dive into Bitcoin in the Age

ofCryptocurrency

Leonard Eddison

© Copyright 2017 by Leonard Eddison

All rights reserved.

This document is geared towards providing exact and reliable information with regards to the topic and issue covered. The publication is sold with the idea that the publisher is not required to render accounting, officially permitted, or otherwise, qualified services. If advice is necessary, legal or professional, a practiced individual in the profession should be ordered.

- From a Declaration of Principles which was accepted and approved equally by a Committee of the American Bar Association and a Committee of Publishers and Associations.

In no way is it legal to reproduce, duplicate, or transmit any part of this document in either electronic means or in printed format. Recording of this publication is strictly prohibited and any storage of this document is not allowed unless with written permission from the publisher. All rights reserved.

The information provided herein is stated to be truthful and consistent, in that any liability, in terms of inattention or otherwise, by any usage or abuse of any policies, processes, or directions contained within is the solitary and utter responsibility of the recipient reader. Under no circumstances will any legal responsibility or blame be held against the publisher for any reparation, damages, or monetary loss due to the information herein, either directly or indirectly.

Respective authors own all copyrights not held by the publisher.

The information herein is offered for informational purposes solely, and is universal as so. The presentation of the information is without contract or any type of guarantee assurance.
The trademarks that are used are without any consent, and the publication of the trademark is without permission or backing by the trademark owner. All trademarks and brands within this book are for clarifying purposes only

and are the owned by the owners themselves, not affiliated with this document.

Introduction

Thank you and congratulations for downloading *Bitcoin: A Deep Dive into Bitcoin in the Age of Cryptocurrency*. This book was written to assist anyone who is interested in learning about bitcoin and how it has introduced us to the world of cryptocurrencies.

Throughout this book you can expect to learn more about what bitcoinis, specifically, how it works, technical aspects of this cryptocurrency, what we have learned as a result of bitcoin, and what the future may look with bitcoin and other cryptocurrencies in it. As a result, you will have a thorough understanding of what nearly a decade of bitcoin's existence has taught us as a society.

With this book you can learn everything you need to learn about how this currency works and why you might be interested in it. You will understand how it can be used for purchasing and shopping, why people are interested in investing in it, and why people are continuing to mine it despite the currency having been around for nearly a decade. You will also gain insight as to why people are so excited about this currency and what it could mean for us in the future.

Please enjoy this read as you dive deeper into the world of bitcoin and the technology and advances it has brought along with it. And again, thank you and congratulations on the download!

Chapter 1: Understanding Bitcoin

Bitcoin is a highly unique form of currency that was designed and introduced to the world in the year 2009. After being on the market for just shy of a decade at the time of this publication, there is a lot that we have learned from and have come to understand about bitcoin. Before we explore the incredible world of bitcoin and how it looks and works from a technical standpoint, let's take a moment to develop an understanding of what bitcoin is, specifically.

What is Bitcoin?

Bitcoin is a revolutionary form of currency that was introduced in 2009 by an anonymous developer who introduced the currency under the alias "Satoshi Nakamoto". The introduction of this currency opened us up to the world of cryptocurrencies, or currencies that are entirely based in the digital space. Although there are now other forms of cryptocurrencies available, bitcoin is considered the pioneer and is still the most widely recognized and used cryptocurrency traded on the market.

Like other forms of currency, bitcoins can be used for a variety of different purchasing practices. People can use their bitcoins to purchase anything from webhosting services to pizza, meaning that this currency has been designed to literally replicate and potentially one day replace traditional currency. There are very few differences between bitcoin and traditional currency when we look at it from a basic angle, but if you dive even deeper you will notice that bitcoin has many features that are not currently held by traditional currency.

Why Use Bitcoin?

There are several reasons as to why people may choose to use bitcoin, including the attractive no-fee factor that comes along with digital currency. Bitcoins, as you will soon learn in chapter 2, are not held or owned by any one person prior to being purchased by the marketplace. This means that there are no banks or corporations involved in owning or producing bitcoin. As you will learn in the next chapter, bitcoin was produced using a specific algorithm and therefore are not originally owned by anyone, not even the developer.

Since bitcoin do not require banks or other financial institutions to be involved in any part of the transaction process, people who own bitcoin are not required to provide any identifying evidence about who they are. This means items can be purchased with completely anonymity. The elimination of the third party is also responsible for why you are not required to pay any transaction fees or other bank-related or financial institution-related fees on your funds or transactions.

Another incredible feature associated with bitcoin is that you are not required to pay any additional fees when you are conducting international purchases. Traditional currencies are based on an individual country or region thus meaning that said country is welcome to put any laws on their currency at their own discretion. Bitcoin, on the other hand, is not owned by any particular country or region, therefore no one is capable of making any laws that would increase the fees, apply additional taxes, or otherwise increase the cost of doing business or conducting transactions overseas.

Upon its initial launch many individuals and businesses were wary of bitcoin. It sounded too good to be true and like it may have been a scam or something that would not be sustainable. However, it has proven to withstand longevity and is now being more openly accepted across the globe by individuals and merchants alike. More and more shops are allowing individuals to purchase from them using their bitcoin currency. The reason why it may be increasing in attraction to these merchants is because there are no credit card fees or other fees associated for the transaction, even for business owners. This means their cost of doing business is decreased each time someone uses bitcoin to purchase merchandise, instead of a credit card or otherwise.

Another aspect of bitcoin comes into play when you regard the investment value. Bitcoins have significantly increased in worth since they were initially introduced, and have increased even more since the final one was mined and has thus gone into circulation. There is no longer any potential to mine them for free, thus meaning that the amount existing is the only amount that will ever exist for bitcoin in particular. The increasing value of bitcoin has made them an admirable investment for many individuals. Those who are looking to diversify their investment portfolio or who are looking for something new and potentially massive to invest in are starting to look towards bitcoin. There have even been an influx of investment advisors and facilities established to specifically discuss bitcoin and assist individuals in investing in this digital currency.

How Can You Acquire Bitcoins?

The most well-known way to acquire bitcoins is through computer mining. Although this is not the cheapest or easiest way, it does result in you earning free bitcoin from your mining practices. You will learn plenty more about the specific way the mining is accomplished in chapter 2, but ultimately it is a system of complex mathematical equations that are solved by computers. This is how bitcoins were originally created and how more continue to enter circulation. At the time of this publication there are approximately 25 bitcoins mined every 10 minutes using these complex computers and their mathematical equations.

Another way to get your hands on bitcoins, which is much easier, is to find a bitcoin exchange and simply purchase them. Because of how many of these exchanges exist and the nature of the currency, it is important that you take your time and find an exchange where you will not be scammed. Avoid any company or individual who claims that they will help you mine bitcoin, anything that seems too good to be true, or anything that has a generally bad feel to it. Ideally, you should be able to research the bitcoin exchange in question and discover a great deal of information about it right away. Make sure that you always research the exchange to ensure that you are not being ripped off. Because of how valuable bitcoin is these days, many people are using it as an opportunity to scam individuals out of their funds and you do not want to be a victim. One other thing worth noting is pyramid-schemes that involve bitcoin. While these may sound profitable or like they will assist you with investing, they will not save you money and they will also likely result in you not having any bitcoin in the end.

Despite how many scams exist out there surrounding bitcoin, it is important that you understand that this is not worth completely abandoning the bitcoin currency over.

Recall that even traditional currencies can result in scams, and yet they are still highly valuable and are even essential to daily life in our society. Bitcoins are not as necessary to our daily life, but they are still highly valuable and can provide a great deal of return and wealth to those who purchase them or invest in them.

The best thing to do is ensure that you are using credible and legitimate sources from which to purchase your bitcoin. Once you have identified a sound exchange to invest in, you can begin freely investing in as many bitcoin as you desire. This is the easiest and safest way to become involved in owning and trading bitcoin without having to fear that you will be scammed or otherwise ripped off in the world of cryptocurrencies.

Where Are Bitcoins Stored?

Much like traditional currency, bitcoins have a digital "wallet" in which you store them. This wallet is automatically created whenever you purchase your first bitcoin and it is held for you from that point forward. Any time you purchase bitcoin or invest in this cryptocurrency it will be added to your digital wallet. Similarly, any time you spend the currency it will be withdrawn from this digital wallet.

Your digital wallet exists in one of two places: either directly on your computer, or in the cloud storage system. This wallet operates exactly as your bank would, keeping track of any bitcoin that enter your wallet and any that you leave. You can use this wallet to help you when it comes to paying for goods, receiving or sending funds, or even saving your bitcoin funds.

It is important to understand, however, that there are some dangers that can be faced with your digital wallet that are not reversible should they happen. For example, the wallet is not insured by the FDIC so should you have any discrepancies or lose any of your funds, you will not be able to retrieve them or revive them with the help of insurance. Furthermore, there are things worth noting about where you choose to store the wallet, as well. For wallets that are stored on the cloud, some companies may have the power to take more bitcoin than you have approved or otherwise take your currency. As well, servers could be hacked and the hacker themselves could steal your bitcoin. If you store your wallet on your computer, however, it can be hacked or damaged with viruses, or they could be deleted or lost should your computer ever fail.

Chapter 2: The Technical Side

Since bitcoin is a digital currency that is dealt with entirely online, it is only natural that it has a technical side to it. As you briefly learned in the previous chapter, bitcoins are mined using complex mathematical equations that are solved by computers. In this chapter we are going to explore exactly what this means, the types of equations that are used, the computers required for the mining process, and other technical elements of this currency.

The Creation of Bitcoin

The creation of bitcoin is perhaps one of the most revolutionary technological creations in a long time based on the fact that it is done in a decentralized manner. This means that there is no particular system, computer, or network that is responsible for the creation and distribution of bitcoin. Instead, it is created using a decentralized algorithm that distributes it across a series of networks. This means that no particular network can hack or stop the creation of bitcoin.

Since the bitcoins are created in a decentralized manner, there is a process known as mining that is responsible for essentially "identifying" bitcoin and bringing them into creation. The process of mining results in a series of individuals who have designed computers and software that mine bitcoin. They are then rewarded with the bitcoins themselves. Essentially each time a new computer plugs into the mining process they are assisting with the processing of transactions and they are also assisting with securing the network using specialized hardware. Because of their contributions to the bitcoin network they are rewarded with bitcoins in exchange, which they can then use at their discretion.

The way the bitcoin algorithm works, they can only be created at a fixed rate. You cannot accelerate or decelerate the speed at which bitcoins are created. Because of this specific factor, bitcoin is a highly competitive business. When more individuals become involved in the mining process they take away some of the profits that were previously being earned by a fewer number of people, thus meaning it is distributed across a wider network and becomes less profitable to the existing network. Because of the decentralized nature of the currency there is no way to control how many miners become involved in the process or how many bitcoins are awarded to any specific miner. There is no way to manipulate the system or otherwise increase your odds of earning more bitcoins than others because any attempts at modifying the system will be shut down by every bitcoin node across the entire world.

One other aspect of bitcoins that is interesting to note is that the algorithm was designed so that the number of bitcoins created each year would be automatically cut in half. This means each year only half the number of bitcoins will be produced as the year before. The process will end when there are approximately 21 million bitcoins in circulation. Once they have capped out there is no way to create any further bitcoin as the algorithm will no longer allow it. There will be no potential for miners or anyone to mine any further bitcoin in the system.

Everything You Should Know About Bitcoin Mining

As you learned previously, the process of mining is essentially the process of creating bitcoins that are then put into circulation. The miners are not only responsible for mining and creating bitcoins, however. Their interaction with the system is also responsible for increasing the computing power involved in processing transactions, as well as securing the network and ensuring that everyone who is involved in the system is synchronized so as to create the decentralized factor of bitcoins.

The term "mining" was used for bitcoins because the process of being involved in this system meant that you would temporarily be rewarded for your involvement. The term was used as an analogy relating the process of being rewarded bitcoins to mining gold, however you should understand that the two processes are not at all similar. When it comes to mining gold you are responsible for digging and finding the gold and as a result you are then "rewarded" with the gold. When it comes to mining bitcoin, however, you are essentially being rewarded for your services to the bitcoin system. In exchange for you increasing the security and computing speed of the decentralized system, you are rewarded with bitcoin. Even once the last bitcoin has been issued and there are no more to be rewarded for mining processes they will still be required to mine, as each mining node is responsible for creating the entire decentralized system that ultimately controls bitcoin itself.

Bitcoin mining can be accomplished by simply having the proper software and specialized hardware. The software itself works by listening to transactions that are being broadcast between the bitcoin's peer-to-peer network and overseeing any tasks that are involved with processing and confirming the transaction to ensure that they are successfully approved and fulfilled. By allowing their specialized hardware to run these software, bitcoin miners are rewarded both with the creation of new bitcoin (for now) as well as a small transaction fee that is paid for by users. Yes, bitcoin miners are paid a small transaction fee, but to clarify, this fee is completely optional. The purpose of the fee is to increase the processing time so that transactions are approved faster. If they do not wish to increase the speed of the transaction, they are not required to pay any fee.

The process of confirming new transactions requires the software to create a "block" that features mathematical proof that the transaction was approved and actually worked. Creating these proofs is extremely difficult because there is only a single way that they can be created, which essentially requires the software to perform billions of calculations per second until it finds the correct one. This means that the software must complete the calculations and identify the correct one before the block can be accepted by the overall network and be rewarded and approved. The average time to find a block is approximately 10 minutes, which never changes. Each time a new miner becomes a part of the network the complexity is automatically increased to maintain this 10-minute time period. This increases the competitiveness associated with bitcoin mining because the more miners that are involved the less chance you have at being the individual that owns the software responsible for creating the new block. As you may recall as well, there are zero ways to increase your odds or improve your chances of being the one responsible for creating the block because there is no individual identity or system that can control what is included on the block chain.

Using the proof of work in each block associated with each transaction is also designed with a specific purpose when it comes to bitcoin technology. While transactions could simply be approved in a matter of minutes based on a simple plus or minus calculation, having this complex system that involves proof of work and forces each transaction into a block ultimately forces the blocks to be issued in chronological order. Because of this block chain pattern, it is extremely difficult to reverse any previous transactions that were made because it would require the entire chain to be recalculated. The proofs associated with that particular block would need to be recalculated and so would all subsequent blocks.

If two blocks were found at the exact same time by miners, the miners would work on the first block that was received and then switch to the longest chain of blocks immediately following the discovery of the next one. This process ensures that the mining practice stays secure.

Based on the block chain technology associated with bitcoin and the decentralized nature of bitcoins there is absolutely zero opportunity for any miner to cheat the system. You cannot increase your reward or otherwise manipulate the system in any way because the entire system would shut down the transaction. There is no way to corrupt the bitcoin network because if all nodes are not in agreement with any particular transaction it is completely declined by the entire network. In order for anything to be approved it must be proofed and then entered into the entire system. If one system was not in agreement with the rest of the systems on the network, then the transaction would be denied by the entire network. It would never be entered as a block and no funds would be traded from one party to the next. Because of this very feature you can ensure that all bitcoin miners are trusted and should not raise any need for suspicion.

How Bitcoin Introduced the Block Chain Technology

As you read in the previous section, block chain was introduced at the same time bitcoin was introduced. It wasn't until after bitcoin was launched, however, that developers discovered the power of block chain technology and the potential it has to change the way many online activities take place.

If you are unaware of what block chain is, it is a public ledger that is shared by anyone who desires to look into it. Bitcoin operates on the block chain as a means to permanently record transactions that take place. If you will recall, transactions are hashed into "blocks" which are then put on the chronological chain. They are virtually impossible to eliminate from the chain once they have been stored there, so anything that is entered onto the block chain exists permanently on that unique chain.

Block chain is a technology that has the power to transform the transparency of the online community. This is particularly interesting when it comes to the idea of creating transparency between companies and the public, as well as government and the public.

Block chain was the primary development alongside bitcoin that made the entire process work. Although bitcoin is the currency and the main topic when people talk about this cryptocurrency, block chain is the behind-the-scenes technology that brings bitcoin to life. Without it, transactions would not be possible, nor would the development of new bitcoins. Instead, bitcoin would merely be a theory and there would be nothing that makes it work. Alternatively, it may have been built on an independent server which would have made it insecure and ultimately likely caused the entire development to fail. Block chain enabled bitcoin developers to generate an entire currency that had a decentralized platform to share it between individuals and to keep the transactions transparent and secure.

From a technological stand point, bitcoin and block chain have been two of the most incredible discoveries in a long time. When they were developed they opened us up to an entirely new world of possibilities, including cryptocurrencies and secure and transparent transactions. Although they are the first of their kind, the development of these two technologies have already paved the way for several more incredible developments to exist within' the technological realm of currencies and transactions. You will learn more about bitcoin as a currency in chapter 3, and more about what we have learned as a result of these two developments in chapter 4.

Chapter 3: Bitcoin as A Currency

The technological side of bitcoin is the "behind-the-scenes" look, which you learned about in chapter 2. However, the entire purpose of bitcoin was that it was to be used as a digital form of currency. In this chapter you are going to explore exactly how bitcoin works as a currency and why it has become so popular. You will also discover why so many people are attracted to this unique form of currency.

How Do You Make a Bitcoin Payment?

Conducting payments with your bitcoin application is significantly easier than paying through virtually any other means. It is the easiest way to pay for something online to date. In order to send a payment through bitcoin, you simply open your bitcoinwallet application, enter the recipient's bitcoin address, key in the desired payment amount and then hit send. If you prefer, you can also scan the merchant's QR code or tap your smartphones together using NFC technology to conduct the transaction.

Using bitcoin is similar to using PayPal funds, only you never have to enter your banking information or otherwise identify yourself beyond using your bitcoin address. Once you have chosen how much to send and hit send, the transaction is complete and the only remaining part of the process is to allow for it to send and be confirmed by the miners.

Life Cycle of Bitcoin Transactions

The lifecycle of bitcoin transactions is slightly different than traditional currency. With traditional currency you acquire it, it goes into your bank account (or wallet), and you spend it. It is gone. You may receive a receipt that confirms the funds were received by the recipient, or you may not.

Bitcoin's transaction life cycles are different from this. As a merchant it starts with your digital wallet, your keypairs, and some bitcoins. You create the transaction using your unspent bitcoins and then it is signed with your private keys. The client will then have a copy of it stored in their own wallet as well. Once you are ready, the client will broadcast the new transaction using the Bitcoin Network, which will then be broadcast to every 8th peer. This ensures that your anonymity is protected, but also that the decentralized platform can approve the transaction. Each client or miner that receives the transaction can scrutinize it to ensure that there are no errors and that no double-spending is taking place. If any of the criteria are failed by the transaction, then it is completely ignored. However, it if meets the criteria then there is a note kept within temporary memory. It will then be broadcast to several more peers to ensure that the transaction can be approved. Depending on the rate you paid for the transaction fee, this process may be quick or it may be slow. The less you paid, or if you avoided fees altogether, then the transaction will be much slower than it would be if you were to pay fees for priority service.

Once the transaction passes the peers and clients it then reaches what is known as mining pools, which essentially represents the network of mining computers that form the foundation of the decentralized platform for bitcoin. Here, it will be recognized and then included in every block that is created going forward. Although it will be stored, it will be recognized as 0 confirmations until one of the miners is able to approve the transaction and it is officially confirmed in the block chain. The only purpose of each individual miner at this point is to crunch numbers and make a proof of the transaction, not to check for the validity of your block. That will happen later by the entire mining pool.

Once a block is effectively solved your transaction will be included within' that block. Then, it will be broadcast to all of the peers throughout the bitcoin network where it will be kept in a note from now on, as a part of the permanent block chain. This means your transaction now has 1 confirmation, and it will be stored forever to ensure that no double-spending takes place. Over the next few transactions yours will be included in each subsequent block, which each counts as 1 additional confirmation. Once the transaction reaches six or more confirmations it is considered fully confirmed and your transaction is complete.

Although the transaction is complete, the lifecycle of the bitcoin is not actually complete. It will only be completed once it is spent by a subsequent transaction, which means that its outputs will then be forgotten from the "unspent" memory and any further attempt to spend these bitcoins will be disregarded completely. However, the memory of the transaction itself will be permanently hashed into the block chain, so long as people are willing to keep track of the entire chain through the mining pools and bitcoin network.

Because of how long the life cycle of a bitcoin transaction is, it is natural that the transactions can take quite some time to approve. This is why there are fees associated with spending and receiving bitcoins. The more you pay for your fee, the more priority your transaction will take in the network and therefore the faster it will be approved - or disregarded. However, the less you pay or if you choose not to pay at all, the process will take significantly longer as you will fall to the bottom of the list and others will take priority over yours.

Why Do Bitcoins Have Value?

When bitcoins were introduced, they were introduced as a form of currency. As a result, they have been viewed as a form of currency ever since. Bitcoins, despite not being a physical currency, have all of the same values and benefits of any other currency. Unlike others, however, they are backed by mathematics instead of physical properties.

These reasons alone, however, are not enough to justify why bitcoin holds value. The true reason why they are considered valuable is because people have entrusted them and adopted them in as a true form of currency. This means that people have placed value on them and therefore they have become valuable. Bitcoin's value is determined by and raised by the increasing number of users including merchants and startups that are using bitcoin in their financial plans. Like any other currency that exists, bitcoin's value comes from people's willingness to accept it as a form of payment in return for services or goods.

What Determines Bitcoin's Price?

Similar to other commodities and currencies, the price of each bitcoin is based directly on supply and demand. The more that people purchase bitcoin and get into the idea of using bitcoin as a currency, the higher the value of each bitcoin goes up. However, when people are less interested in it or are not using it as often, the value goes down. Unlike other currencies, however, bitcoin's value is extremely volatile. Other currencies are created in a controlled amount, but can be created when it is needed. However, bitcoin is created at a very predictable and decreasing rate. As you know there are only about 21 million that will ever exist, which means the market is incredibly small compared to other forms of currency. This means that very small amounts of monetary changes can significantly affect the value of each bitcoin.

Some people fear that bitcoin will fail and lose all of its value altogether, but it is important to look at history when we consider this element. In the past there have been many different currencies that were introduced and failed, or that slowly faded away over time. Unlike those currencies, however, bitcoin has always held a fairly steady value in the market. It is important to understand, still, that bitcoin could eventually fade away and cease to exist any longer. Political issues, lack of demand, or even a major technical failure could lead to bitcoin failing altogether. This is true for any currency, however, and paying attention to the market and the value of the currency itself is a great way to predict how and where it is going. For now, it stays rather stable over its long-term market value, despite being such a volatile market.

Security Features

Because of the decentralized nature of bitcoin and the protocol and cryptography behind the currency, bitcoin is known to have a strong security system. The bitcoin network is distributed across the entire globe and yet it remains an incredibly secure system for the cryptocurrency to exist on.

The primary security failure experienced with bitcoin is when users make an error in their usage of the network. Breaches of your individual computer or cloud network could result in your private keys being lost or stolen, or you may accidentally delete the files and thus lose all of your bitcoins and your entire address associated with your account. However, there are ways to avoid running into any user-based errors that could result in your currency being compromised. For example, being careful with online services to avoid viruses, keeping smaller amounts in your wallet and keeping the rest stored in a bitcoin savings account, backing up your wallet, encrypting your wallet to protect it from thieves, and having an offline wallet for your bitcoin savings are all great ways to protect your currency. Furthermore, keeping your software up to date on the devices where your currency is stored and using the multi-signature feature to protect against theft are also excellent solutions.

The bitcoin network itself is a relatively safe network that has had very little problems since its launch. Because of the nature of it, any hacks are typically identified rapidly and therefore anything that occurred during the breach can be restored. However, anything that has been done by the user on their independent computer outside of the network cannot be resolved. So, if you delete your files or your individual computer is hacked by a virus, anything lost cannot be recovered, not even using the decentralized network. Using security features such as those listed in the previous paragraph are the best opportunity you have to protect your funds and ensure that nothing is lost.

Advantages

We covered some of the benefits of bitcoin in chapter 1, but now you can develop a deeper understanding about all of the advantages associated with bitcoin. As we have already discussed, payment freedom is a big one. Being able to conduct international transactions without being interrupted by government, holidays, banks, or other interruptions is an incredible feature that makes conducting transactions significantly quicker for those who are looking to purchase things from an international merchant.

Another benefit we have already discussed is the opportunity to choose your own fees. You can choose to pay as much or as little as you want, even nothing, when it comes to conducting transactions with your bitcoins. The only thing affected by your fees is the speed at which the transaction is conducted.

The anonymity of bitcoin means that both merchants and customers are protected when it comes to bitcoin. The transactions are irreversible which means that a customer cannot pay for something, receive their item and then later reverse the transaction and receive their funds back. Believe it or not this is a popular scamming method that is used by many people with debit cards and credit cards. Bitcoin uses block chain which permanently recognizes the transaction, thus making it irreversible. Furthermore, being anonymous means that the sensitive information of both the client and the merchant is completely hidden in regards to the transaction. Only basic information regarding the transaction is stored permanently on the block chain.

With other payment methods, merchants actually have the power to force fees that were not wanted or known about by the client. Using bitcoin, this is virtually impossible. Without the insertion of the client's private key, no funds can be taken. This means that your money as a consumer is protected because no one can access it without your specific information, even if you have already provided them with access to your funds through a previous transaction. They can take the approved amount, period. Nothing more, nothing less.

Finally, all information regarding transactions is controlled by the block chain and is therefore completely transparent and neutral. Although personal information is not associated with transactions, identification keys are. These are not private keys, but rather the block chain and bitcoin protocol's method of knowing "who" made the purchase. While the public cannot see what your name is or your sensitive information associated with the transaction, they can see your transaction if they so choose. This means that all transactions can be identified and confirmed by the public eye, ensuring that your cryptocurrency transactions maintain their security.

Disadvantages

Despite being an incredible form of currency, there are actually still many disadvantages associated with bitcoin. These disadvantages do somewhat affect the value of them, as well as how efficient and effective they are for those who choose to use them.

The first and biggest disadvantage is the degree of acceptance. Although the number of merchants accepting payments through bitcoin is rapidly growing, they are still not widely recognized like traditional currency is. This means that you are not able to use your bitcoin anywhere, despite the fact that in theory it would work perfectly. The more this list grows, the more the network will benefit from it and the more bitcoin value will likely continue to increase as the supply and demand will naturally increase as well.

Another reason why bitcoin is not always the best currency to be invested in is because of their volatility. Since the value is still extremely small from what they could be, and they are rapidly changing, it can make using bitcoin incredibly hard. You may have a certain value one day and significantly less the next day based on volatility alone. This can make using them unpredictable and frustrating.

Finally, bitcoin software is actually still considered to be in beta phase despite having been launched for nearly a decade now. This means that many of the features that are associated with bitcoin are not actually active yet. As the software is continually developed we will begin to see more tools, features, and services that are offered for bitcoin users. Furthermore, we will likely see the introduction of insurances and other additional security features that will increase the quality of the service. As this happens, bitcoin will mature and may find itself as a candidate for the next form of currency that will be widely used and accepted by society.

Is Bitcoin an Asset or a Currency?

As we discuss bitcoin as a currency, it is important that we address a common misconception that is floating around the internet these days. Many individuals purchase bitcoin as an investment option. They simply sit on their bitcoin until the market turns in their favor and then sell them for a great profit. While this is certainly one way that bitcoin can be used, it is not the only way. Still, many people argue that because this is one of the most popular forms of bitcoin being used that it is an asset instead of a currency.

Something to understand is that assets are not typically spent in exchange for products or services from merchants. However, currencies are. Likewise, many currencies are traded as stocks in the market and it is important to understand that bitcoin falls within' this realm of currency.

Even though it is a significantly smaller market and features significantly fewer "dollars" than most currencies do, it is still a currency. You store it in a "wallet" and spend it on goods and services which ultimately defines it as a currency.

Still, you can use bitcoin as an asset as well. However, the idea that bitcoin is only an asset was likely introduced by investors who are attempting to focus on the investment factors of bitcoin. These are also likely people who are skeptical about the currency and its potential to become widely used by merchants and consumers. Although it has not become nearly as popular as other forms of currency, it is still growing in maturity and therefore people should recognize that it is not yet at its fullest potential. In time we will likely see many more merchants accepting bitcoin as a form of payment and therefore it will increase in popularity as a currency as much as it has as an asset.

Chapter 4: What Bitcoin Has Taught Us

The introduction of bitcoin has taught us a great deal about currency, financial institutions, and even consumers. This information helps us identify a lot about currency itself, markets, and even the way the future could (and should) look based on the experience we gain with bitcoin, among other cryptocurrencies. In this chapter we are going to explore everything that we have learned since the development and introduction of bitcoin.

There is a Legitimate Alternative to Centrally Managed Systems

The biggest thing we need to pay attention to and perhaps the biggest lesson we have learned as a result of the introduction of bitcoin is the fact that there is a legitimate alternative to centrally managed systems that are already in use by modern society. The modern methods for managing money involve financial institutions that are centrally managed, namely banks. Although banks have served us in an incredible way, they are also not the best when it comes to choosing how to manage something as important to our society as currencies. Banks have many flaws to them, including the fact that they are not the most secure method of storing and using money. There are many ways that transactions can be done without permission, they are not transparent, and they can also have their funds stolen through hacking accounts or scammers otherwise gaining unlawful access to your financial resources. Bitcoin, however, contains many security features that keep your funds safe and protected while also making transactions transparent and protecting you from having your funds stolen or otherwise hacked. While viruses and other forms of malware can still pose a threat to your bitcoin funds, further testing and maturing of the bitcoin currency will likely introduce newer and more secure methods of protecting your funds so that they are completely safe from being stolen or hacked.

Furthermore, keeping funds in a bitcoin wallet and conducting transactions peer-to-peer through bitcoin gives users the choice to eliminate transaction fees altogether if they so desire. This means that we are no longer forced to pay in order to store and manage our funds within one centrally located facility. Instead, we can manage them on our own and choose to pay only if we desire and only for accelerated services. Should we choose not to pay we are still entitled to the same services, they will simply take slightly longer to be fulfilled.

Ultimately, bitcoin has taught us that there is no need for us to rely entirely on centralized facilities to use currencies. While it will likely be a long time before we see decentralized cryptocurrencies completely eliminate the need for traditional currency altogether, it is not unlikely that it could happen eventually. Once the software is completely worked out and tested to ensure that it is functional and reliable it is likely that we will see bitcoin become even more popular, thus making it a possibility that cryptocurrency could eventually be the main form of currency that we rely on.

Each Currency Exists with Strengths and Weaknesses

Bitcoin has pushed the conversation on currencies into the public eye and has had many speculators discussing the strengths and weaknesses of currency altogether. Up until the introduction of bitcoin, it had been a long time since we had any credible reason to challenge the idea of traditional currencies. Now, however, there are many speculators who have strong opinions about the many advantages and disadvantages of each unique form of currency. The common consensus is that each form, traditional currency and cryptocurrency, comes with its own set of advantages and disadvantages. However, this means that we can further explore these advantages and disadvantages and potentially make them a topic in the development of further cryptocurrencies. Since cryptocurrencies are new and presently in development stages, it means that there is a significant amount of opportunity for developers to work towards minimizing the disadvantages and making cryptocurrency much stronger and much more beneficial than traditional currencies, for consumers, corporations, and for government bodies.

To further explore the common consensus on the strengths and weaknesses of each unique type of currency, let's dive deeper into what people are saying about each form. For digital currencies or cryptocurrencies, it is generally agreed upon that the ability to have easy international transactions and lower transaction costs altogether is extremely attractive. Furthermore, the transparency of the currency, the security of it, and the fact that you can remain anonymous with your purchases are all admirable traits that are carried by bitcoin. However, many speculate that the fact that it is not widely accepted and that it is still in developmental stages makes it unreliable or unattractive to the average person. Furthermore, the fact that the value of the bitcoin is constantly fluctuating means that the value of the currency you are holding could be worth a significantly higher amount one day than it is the next, meaning that it is not presently a reliable daily-use currency.

On the other hand, traditional currencies come with their own set of strengths and weaknesses as well. For example, they are widely accepted and have been used for many years therefore they are reliable and predictable. You are not going to have the value fluctuate significantly overnight, and if it does it is typically able to be predicted based on the present economic state or changes in governing bodies. However, traditional currency is not always as secure as digital currency. To elaborate, it is not as secure as digital currency is *strictly based on the system and not the individual user.* Unlike the decentralized system associated with bitcoin and other cryptocurrencies, centralized systems can be hacked and manipulated as you have already learned. This means that using banks or other financial institutions is not always the safest option when it comes to using your money. Although we all tend to rely on and entrust our banks with our money, it does not necessarily mean that it is in the safest place or that it is not able to be stolen or otherwise syphoned from our accounts. Still, it is the best option we have to date so most of us rely on banks and other financial institutions to help us manage our finances.

Valuation of Bitcoin Is Complex

When it comes to the valuation of bitcoin there are typically two that people pay attention to: the present valuation of the cryptocurrency, and the future valuation of the cryptocurrency. Obviously, the present valuation is a real-time valuation that represents what the money is actually worth. This is the most important number as this is the one that identifies what your purchasing power is based on the funds you have in your digital wallet. However, many people like to focus on the future valuation as well. This number is not set in stone and cannot be accurately predicted no matter how hard we try, but many believe that as bitcoin increases in popularity and reaches maturity it will likely become worth much more money.

Because of the differences between present valuation and future valuation when it comes to bitcoin it makes the valuation process difficult. Many people purchase bitcoin now as an investment with the belief that it will be worth significantly more in the future. However, there is no way to guarantee this. In the meantime, bitcoin is a highly volatile currency that is heavily influenced by the number of people that invest in it and the number of people that are willing to accept it as payment.

With currency there are two types of activities that affect its value: those that increase it and those that decrease it. Simple, right? For bitcoin there are three primary activities that increase the value of bitcoins and three that decrease the value. Those that increase it include replenishing your digital wallet, paying merchants using bitcoins, and paying salaries or wages using bitcoins. When this is done with bitcoin it increases the perceived value of the bitcoin therefore making them worth much more per piece. However, when miners cash out their earnings, users redeem bitcoins for local currencies, or those who are paid wages in bitcoin convert their bitcoin to local currencies, the value of the bitcoin decreases. This is because it is no longer being used or the perceived usability of it is lower and therefore the value itself becomes significantly lower.

For those who are heavily invested in bitcoin, including those who purchase into it and those who are in the process of advancing the development of it, the hope is that bitcoin will continue to increase in value. The more it increases, the more credible it becomes as a legitimate alternative to traditional currency and therefore the further its popularity will increase. The more it's popularity increases, the higher the supply and demand value becomes and therefore the higher its value goes. It is a cycle that, if spun in the right direction, could result in bitcoin being worth a great deal of money. This is exactly what people are hoping for and working towards and is a large part of the reason as to why we each need to work towards educating ourselves on digital currencies such as bitcoin, as well as how they could be an advantage to our society. The more we are educated, the better a decision we can make regarding cryptocurrencies and therefore the more likely we will be to have cryptocurrencies such as bitcoin that are eventually accepted as a true form of currency and are not regarded as a beta or a prototype for the future of digital currencies. Additionally, the more we are educated the more we can discuss the advantages and disadvantages of currencies and hopefully produce new ones that contain many fewer disadvantages than those that already exist.

Digital Currency Could be a Fact of the Future

As we have had the opportunity to explore the idea of digital currency more in-depth since the launch of bitcoin, it has become increasingly apparent that digital currency could be a fact of the future. Over the course of many years, currency has evolved in several different ways. With the introduction of the digital age came many speculations on how our world may look with a digital future. One of those speculations was the idea of digital currency. The idea of digital currency became partially true when bank cards were introduced and individuals had the power to use a single card to access their funds and process transactions. However, this was only the first step. Introducing bitcoin, as well as other cryptocurrencies that have been developed since the introduction of bitcoin have paved the way for an entirely new outlook for the future of currency and how it may look in a few years' time.

Although it is unlikely that digital currency will become the primary form of currency any time soon, it is clear that there is a really good chance that this could be the future of all currencies. With the number of benefits that are held by cryptocurrency and the very fact that we are in such a powerful position to be able to control the number of advantages and disadvantages that this unique new currency has, there is a good chance that once it is perfected and this form of currency matures well enough, many people may turn to cryptocurrencies like bitcoin and away from traditional currencies.

Of course, there is always the chance that government or other circumstances could result in cryptocurrencies being shut down before that happens, there is a theory and the potential that this could be the face of currency in a few decades' time. The only way we will know for sure is to wait and see. However, based on the amount we have learned from bitcoin and bitcoin protocol, as well as how people are interacting with it and using it, it is clear that many people are highly on board with such an idea and would likely be in support of cryptocurrencies becoming the future of currency in general.

Society Appreciates Having an Alternative

After having been available for nearly a decade, bitcoin has become a popular alternative for many consumers and merchants. The larger the list of merchants who accept bitcoin grows, the more consumers are interested in using it. The growing interest from both parties proves that consumers and merchants alike appreciate the idea of having an alternative option for their funds. Giving society the option and seeing that they willingly choose and advocate for the alternative choice, in this case bitcoin, proves that it is a concept that would likely be welcomed by most of society. While there are always groups of people who would disagree or who would not be interested in using it, a large percentage of the population are interested in the concept and would be willing to keep it going as a permanent structure, perhaps even choosing to use it in place of traditional currency altogether.

Although this piece of information may be seemingly small to many, it is actually a highly valuable piece of information that contributes a great deal to the process of bitcoin maturing as a legitimate currency. If it were introduced and very few people were interested, or if the concept flopped altogether at some point along the way, it would prove that there is no need to continue developing the bitcoin protocol beta in order to turn it into a credible and useable currency that will hopefully be more widely accepted in the future. After all, if society itself wasn't willing to accept the idea then it would never be used for what it's intended purpose was, therefore it would be a waste of time for virtually everyone involved.

Paved the Way for Other Cryptocurrencies

In addition to bitcoin being an incredible and innovative concept that was launched to the public, it has also become a pioneer for the world of cryptocurrencies. While it is the first known cryptocurrency that was introduced to the public, it no longer stands to be the only one. Since the introduction of bitcoin in 2009, several other cryptocurrencies have emerged. This is an amazing piece of information for a variety of reasons.

First and foremost, this means that cryptocurrencies are truly being taken seriously. The very fact enough people are interested in the idea for other developers to even consider coming up with their own unique cryptocurrency proves how serious society is about this alternative from three different angles: consumers, merchants, and developers. The more that people generate interest in cryptocurrencies through talking about them and educating others on them, the more popular they become and therefore the more legitimate they become. This means that more and more people are on board with the idea and that they truly have a strong potential to become a new form of currency that we may eventually use in day-to-day society. Ultimately, it is a great indicator that cryptocurrencies are here to stay and that, we should be prepared to see them eventually become a major part of our society at some point in the future.

The second reason why the emergence of new cryptocurrencies is so incredible is that this means that developers are actively seeking for a form of cryptocurrency that works efficiently enough to actually become a viable alternative to traditional currency. While bitcoin is an incredible alternative, there are some disadvantages that come along with it. The primary disadvantage is how slow it can be when it comes to processing transactions, as well as how few people accept it as a form of payment.

If developers continue researching cryptocurrencies, they are much more likely to discover a form of it that works quickly and seamlessly and that can actually be used as a true alternative to traditional currency. Instead of being an interesting and quirky alternative that may be used from time to time but isn't taken completely seriously just yet, cryptocurrency could become a legitimate alternative that you could use at virtually any merchant in order to purchase goods and services. It could even be used for payrolls and salaries, and other currency-based activities. In fact, we may even see people converting local currency to a cryptocurrency if the market were to grow large enough.

Having several more developers on hand and seeing many different cryptocurrencies emerge into the market is a positive thing in terms of the future of cryptocurrency. It proves even more that cryptocurrency is here to stay and that it truly is a fact of life now, and in the future.

Teaches Us About Currency Itself

Aside from what we have learned specifically about digital currency, bitcoin has also helped us learn more about currency itself. Since the introduction of bitcoin, we have learned a great deal about why currency works and how it works. We have discovered that the primary reason it works is because people place value on it. When people are willing to use it, accept it, and trade it, then it is a viable currency that can be successfully relied upon and therefore used in more common circumstances. When the currency is not commonly accepted as a form of payment, as a method of purchasing goods or services, or as something that could be otherwise traded, then it loses value as a currency. Currency primarily holds value because people give it value. Furthermore, existing currencies are not the only kind that will ever exist. The introduction of a new currency that has been capable of accumulating enough worth that it once held a value of over $4,000 per coin proves new currencies can be introduced and individuals can place value on them, even if they are not entirely tested and are still relatively young and new to the marketplace.

Chapter 5: The Future of Bitcoin Itself

As we continue developing the beta protocol for bitcoin and more information about it comes to light, many people are wondering what the future of bitcoin itself will be. Furthermore, they are wondering about what the future of cryptocurrency looks like. In this chapter we are going to explore what developers have planned for the future of bitcoin and where they hope this currency will end up, eventually.

Bitcoin Protocol Evolves

As developers look to the future and what still lies in store for bitcoin, many are simply focused on the protocol evolving. The more they develop on it and the further the testing goes, the more features and additions they are able to embed into bitcoin protocol. The idea is to add greater security features, while also working out some of the problems that people have when using bitcoin. For example, increasing transaction speed and making the purchasing process more efficient for users.

Evolving bitcoin protocol is ultimately what will take it from a concept and a test into a mature currency. As the protocol itself matures, it will make using the coin significantly easier, therefore increasing the likelihood of people fostering it as a primary currency.

Furthermore, as bitcoin protocol evolves there is always the chance that a newer and better cryptocurrency could emerge in its path and thus take over the cryptocurrency world. If you take a look at virtually any other form of technology throughout history, there has always been some new and improved version that was later shared with the world and ultimately took the place of the initial version. While many additional cryptocurrencies have been introduced since the development of bitcoin, none have been good enough to completely take the limelight and become the ultimate cryptocurrency to deal in. However, this doesn't mean that one couldn't be created and replace bitcoin in the world of cryptocurrency.

Buying Process is Made Easier

At the present time, acquiring bitcoin is only possible through mining or through purchasing them at a bitcoin exchange. Since not everyone is interested in having heavy duty equipment that is capable of mining bitcoin, the common opportunity for people to acquire bitcoin is through an exchange. The idea with the future of bitcoin is to make them easier to acquire, without having to purchase them on an exchange website. How this would be made possible is entirely unknown at this point, but many are speculating that they will eventually introduce a feature where you can seamlessly convert local currencies into bitcoin currency. However, this would only happen if bitcoin was accepted as a primary form of currency, which brings us to our next point.

Accepted as a Primary Currency

The hope for bitcoin to be accepted as a primary currency is ultimately what has developers continuing to work on developing bitcoin protocol. Because the potential for bitcoin to be accepted as a primary currency is so high, developers continue to work towards finding a way to make it feasible as a primary currency. By working out the issues that people run into and making it a more stable currency, developers can increase the likelihood that more people and localities will foster it as a form of primary currency. This means that you would consider it to be on par with many other currencies, such as the USD or CAD. By having bitcoin available as a primary currency, this would ultimately open us up to designing the world that would feature some of the inventions as outlined in the next chapter about what a future with bitcoin might mean for our society.

Reduced Volatility

It is no secret that bitcoin is a highly volatile market right now. As people go back and forth between the idea of it becoming a primary currency and more people learn about it, the market continues to swing back and forth. Any primary currency has a much more stable market, meaning that it does not rapidly go back and forth between higher and lower values. If bitcoin were to become a stable currency, it would be much more reliable as a primary currency. Therefore, the hope is that bitcoin's volatility will decrease and it will become a much more reliable currency.

Faster Transaction Speeds

At the moment, some transactions are faster than others. As you already know, the speed of your transaction is based on the fee you pay upon the transaction. Those who pay a higher fee have their transaction prioritized. However, this means that those who pay a lower fee are waiting an enormous amount of time for their transactions to be processed. In fact, even many of the individuals who pay higher fees wait a large amount of time. As developers work towards increasing the usability of bitcoin, they are faced with the task of making the coin easier to conduct transactions with. The goal would be to have a currency where the transaction would be just as quick as using your debit or credit card. This would make it much more efficient, therefore increasing the attractiveness of the currency and making individuals more likely to use it, rather than just hoard it.

Usable for Everyday Purchases

Once bitcoin was accepted as a primary currency, the transaction speeds were increased, and the coin itself was reliable, developers fantasize that bitcoin would be usable for daily purchases. This means any purchase you would conduct online could be conducted using bitcoin itself. Additionally, they may discover ways to use it for in-person merchant purchases as well. Using bitcoin for a day-to-day shopping life would mean that the currency had fully integrated into our currency lineup, thus making this the ultimate action that would prove that bitcoin was accepted as a primary currency form.

The Potential for New Technology Altogether

As a result of bitcoin, we were introduced to block chain technology. Each are interrelated but are known to be valuable for two different reasons. While one can't rely without the other, the two also serve as independent technologies that have opened the realm of opportunity for further experiments and development on both ends. Block chain has the potential to provide us with additional technologies that incorporate block chain into their development and bitcoin provides us with the potential for a future with cryptocurrencies. However, just because these are the two discoveries and realizations at the moment doesn't mean that further technology couldn't be discovered as a result of developing upon them.

When we learn about new technologies such as these two, further development can often lead us to further discoveries. This means that as a result of the development of bitcoin and block chain, we may discover an entirely new realm of possibility that could lend itself to the future of our society. Based on these two technologies, the way we approach technology as a whole, the capabilities of our devices, and how our society operates could all be changed. While this is not guaranteed, it certainly is a potential reality when we explore the realm of possibilities.

Knowing the exact future of where bitcoin will end up versus where developers and society hopes it will end up is difficult. Naturally, with developers regularly working towards improving the currency so that it can be a feasible alternative, it is expected that it will at the very least develop into something beyond the concept and interest that it is today. However, as the development continues we may discover new alternatives or options that arise which are inspired by bitcoin itself. Alternatively, we may discover that bitcoin withstands the test of time and becomes the currency that everyone turns to when it comes to cryptocurrency. It is hard to say with certainty, but one thing remains true regardless of where the exact future lies: we will only know that it has been a successful experiment once bitcoin or an alternative cryptocurrency is officially integrated and accepted as a primary currency.

Chapter 6: A Future with Bitcoin

Based on what we already know, there has been much speculation on what the future might look like if bitcoin or any other cryptocurrency were to stick around and become a primary currency. If bitcoin or any other cryptocurrency were to become a more prominent form of currency, it is no doubt that the world itself would look much different than it does already. Although it may seem like digital currency would simply replace traditional currency and the world would move on as if nothing ever changed, the reality is that cryptocurrency would open up the opportunity for many new advances and developments to come along.

In this chapter we are going to explore what the future may look like if cryptocurrency were to become a primary form of currency that people relied on and used on a regular basis. This will give you an idea of how truly incredible and revolutionary cryptocurrencies actually are and what they could potentially mean for the future of currency, and society as a whole.

Faster and Cost-Effective Bank Transfers

One common complaint regarding banks being our primary financial institutions is the exorbitant fees we are forced to pay on various services. One of the most expensive fees, aside from interest payments and monthly fees on certain institutions, is the cost associated with conducting bank transfers. Transferring money from one bank to another, especially when that transfer is going over a boarder, can be incredibly expensive.

In addition to the fees, banks also take an extremely lengthy amount of time to make the transfer. Instead of simply allowing the transfer to pass from one account to the next, it has to clear houses and corresponding banks prior to actually being deposited into the account of the individual or corporation that it has been sent to. This process is both slow and archaic when you think about it.

A future that involved cryptocurrencies as primary currencies would enable these fees to be eliminated altogether, and it would speed up the process of conducting and approving the transfer. First, the users would be allowed to choose how much they wanted to pay, if anything at all. For those who wanted priority service, they could pay a higher fee to conduct the transfer. Unless, of course, the cryptocurrency in question was efficient enough that this part of the process was no longer relevant. In that case, there would be absolutely no need or temptation to pay fees for any reason. Additionally, the computer system itself would be able to recognize and approve the transfer, therefore eliminating the need for all of the different clearance processes that are required to facilitate these transfers in the current age. Essentially you would have the opportunity to pay virtually nothing to transfer funds, and the transfer would be approved within a matter of hours, if not right away. This would mean that we would both save money and time, and our funds would reach their desired destination in a much quicker fashion.

Increase in Global Remittances

Although this may not be common knowledge for everyone, and it may be irrelevant to many, being able to increase global remittances would mean big things for a lot of people in developing countries. At this time, more than

$500 billion in remittances are sent to third world and developing countries. This number represents the funds being sent back to families by those who move to and settle in western countries. As you can expect, the fees they are paying on these remittances are insanely high, often ranging anywhere from 6% up to 10%. This means that a great deal of the money that could have been sent to and spent by their families is instead being used to pay for the fees just to get the money to their families in the first place.

If bitcoin or an alternative cryptocurrency were to become a primary currency, these fees would be eliminated. Migrants would have the opportunity to send significantly higher amounts of money back to their families, instead of spending it on unnecessary fees. The burden of how much they would have to make in order to support their family would be minimized, and they would have the choice to stop working so hard to make as much *or* send larger amounts of money back to their family. Naturally, these higher amounts being sent back would mean more finances and wealth circulating in these developing countries, thus easing the burden of poverty off of their families.

Cryptocurrency has the power to save migrants and their families thousands of dollars every single year. Allowing them access to a currency that would save them money in fees and increase the amount of money they could potentially send home would be massive for both these migrants and their families. Imagine what difference they could make with an additional 6% to 10% on the money being sent home?

Safe Money for Developing Countries

As you may be aware of, having money in developing countries isn't always safe. With so many living in poverty, it is not unheard of for those living with more wealth than the average populous to be robbed and have their wealth stolen. This is a problem especially with traditional currency because there are few places that the wealth can be stored where it is protected from potential robbery.

In developing countries where mobile technology is growing at a fast pace, such as those in Africa, they are able to store their funds on mobile devices. This is often where the funds are transferred to and from. However, these services can carry fees up to 20% in countries like those in Africa, and they also don't come without risks. This means that users have the choice to store their money on digital accounts and pay outrageous fees, or they have to hold the money in cash and worry about potential robberies resulting in their funds being stolen.

If countries like those in Africa were to have access to cryptocurrencies, however, this would assist in solving their two major problems. There would be zero fees associated with the transactions between individuals, saving them potentially 20% on transfers. There would also be no chance of a robber stealing their cash because there would be no material item to be stolen.

Furthermore, countries like those in Africa and other developing countries face high-inflation risks. Often the worth of their cash becomes less and less as the cost of goods and services increases. While bitcoin or an alternative cryptocurrency would not be entirely free of inflation risks, it would protect them significantly compared to local currencies. That is because local currencies are restricted to the local area, thus meaning that they can easily be impacted by global fluctuations in the economy. Bitcoin, however, would have to fluctuate across the entire globe which would be much less likely. Although bitcoin is a highly volatile currency right now, if it were widely accepted as it would be in order for this benefit to take place, it would likely be more stable than any other currency on the market.

Increased Benefits for E-Commerce

Given that bitcoin is a digital currency, naturally it would have a great deal of benefits for e-commerce businesses. In modern times, e-commerce is rapidly gaining strength and more and more users are turning to e-commerce websites and shops instead of physical store fronts. The number of benefits that both merchants and consumers acquire when they use e-commerce shops is almost incomparable to brick and mortar shops. Although the idea of physically attending a store for the shopping experience is ideal to many, the idea of being able to have everything picked online and delivered directly to your home is increasing in popularity, and therefore becoming far more common.

However, this increase in popularity has not come without risk. The largest risk that consumers and merchants alike face potential fraud that could cost them a significant amount of money. Because of this risk, many are fearful of conducting business with certain merchants or consumers because they do not want to be exposed to the risk. This means that many genuine individuals are being turned away. Although this risk has not slowed down the e-commerce industry as a whole, it has posed as a serious threat to the well-being of many companies. It has also left many consumers reluctant to engage in online shopping activities. If this primary risk was minimized or even eliminated, it is likely that a significantly higher number of people would be engaged in online shopping activities and the e-commerce industry would take off even faster and with much more strength than ever before.

Because bitcoin relies on block chain technology, any transaction that has been processed is virtually impossible to reverse or eliminate. This means that it cannot be undone and therefore people are not able to double spend their money by conducting purchases and then calling their credit card company to reverse the transaction after they have received their shipment. It also makes it significantly easier, safer, and more reliable for merchants to conduct global purchases because they are not at risk of being completely uninsured against these types of fraudulent activities.

Smart Contracts

Smart contracts are a programmable function that enables money to be released when predetermined conditions have been met. These are unlike traditional contracts where two individuals sign an agreement and are legally forced to adhere to said agreement. Instead, two individuals would create an agreement and then a smart contract would be designed. For example, if you have ever seen an online communal freelancing websites where freelancers can connect with potential clients, then you may be aware of the fact that they hold certain funds in escrow while the job is being completed. This means if you hire someone to write a book for you, for example, the company that owns the website itself holds onto the funds while the book is being written. Once the book is marked as complete and both parties agree to this completion, the funds are released to the freelancer. If, however, the book is not marked as complete or the buyer is unhappy with the work or the service, they can deny the completion of the project and they receive their funds back. Essentially the transaction is barred from happening before it even took place.

In a world where this type of service could be offered for virtually anything, it would add an increased amount of protection for both parties involved in funding transactions. When the individual selling a service or good completed their end of the deal, the payment would be guaranteed because it had already been extracted from the seller's account. This would protect them from selling anything and not receiving payment for it as promised, or receiving it significantly later than expected. Likewise, if the good or service was never delivered, the money would be returned to the buyer. They would not have to go through the process of requesting a refund and potentially being denied or completely ignored by the seller. This means that both parties would be protected and funds would be moved at the appropriate time.

This type of smart contract could be offered for many different services. From real estate to the fulfillment and delivery of other large jobs such as construction projects or even website developing projects, smart contracts could be employed to protect both parties and ensure that funds are not an issue. This is far more advanced than present contracts that are written up, as these can only be enforced by law and in many cases there are strategies that either party can use to hide from the law in order to avoid fulfilling their contractual requirements. With a smart contract there would be virtually no way to commit fraud on the other, and the law would never be required in order to settle disputes as disputes would be nonexistent.

Stability for Unstable Currencies

Although some of the leading currencies like the USD, EUR, and CAD are fairly stable, there are still many currencies around the world that are not nearly as mature or stable as these currencies. This means that for these countries who are attempting to nurture these currencies and bring them to maturity, they can often be thrown around by high inflation and volatile market prices.

To give you some insight as to what this looks like exactly, Venezuela has experienced an incredibly high 128% worth of inflation in less than a year. This means that their currency struggles to support their economy and it results in the country itself being forced into poverty on a global scale. Instead of having to attempt to fight to get several younger and less mature currencies to fight with the larger EUR, CAD, USD, and other more stable currencies, one idea would be to introduce a cryptocurrency such as bitcoin. Given that in an ideal world bitcoin would be infinitely more stable, this would give these countries the opportunity to foster a cryptocurrency that was not as volatile and not at risk of plummeting in value like their own currencies have.

Although this may seem like a too-good-to-be-true situation, it may benefit to know that bitcoin has grown seven times more popular in the past year. In fact, in the same year as Venezuela saw 128% increase in their inflation rates. For countries with currencies that are struggling to keep their economy afloat, introducing a global currency like bitcoin could prove to assist these companies and prevent them from experiencing nation-wide poverty.

More Power for the Public

Over the past several decades, people have been forced to place their trust, and their finances, in banks. Based on the way companies and bills are structured, people are not able to choose to keep their money in cash and have no bank accounts. If they do not, they are not able to establish credit with banks and therefore they are typically turned down for different services, right down to the basics such as electricity.

Because of banks having the monopoly over the financial sector and being so heavily involved in many of the basic daily activities we perform, people are forced to do business with them. While this may not seem like much, it does actually reduce the amount of power people have since there truly is no alternative.

If a cryptocurrency were to come to the foreground and become a primary currency, it would provide the public with an alternative to banks and traditional financial institutions. This means that they would have the opportunity to choose an alternative that would still provide them with the means to perform digital transactions, but without all of the attachments, fees, and other drawbacks of a traditional bank system.

Ideally, the functions that can already be performed using your bank's online platform would be replicated in a way, but it would be made more efficient and user friendly. This would include having cheaper and faster services, as well as providing you with more power to decide how you wanted to use and transfer your funds based on your own discretion.

Eliminating the Need for Currency Exchanges

With traditional currencies, exchanges must be made in many instances. When you are conducting business overseas, your local funds must be exchanged to the local funds of the recipient before the business transaction is fully complete. Otherwise, your currency would be unusable to the individual overseas. Likewise, if you were to travel outside of your country, you would have to exchange your currency to the local currency of the place to which you are travelling.

Although these transfers can be done fairly quickly, they are not always ideal. Sometimes one currency may be worth more than the other, therefore meaning you have more or less purchasing power depending on where you are going. Not only is this frustrating in some cases, but it can also cause for tourism to slow down in the country where the purchasing power is out of the consumers favor. Instead, they may choose to go somewhere where their currency is worth more, or just stay home. Not only is this an inconvenience to the consumer, but it can also be difficult for the country itself where their currency is worth less.

In addition to the value of each currency, the cost of exchanging currencies is fairly expensive. This means that you are paying a fairly large fee every time you transfer funds back and forth. For businesses that conduct transactions overseas on a regular basis, consumers trying to purchase online from foreign merchants, and virtually anyone else involved in regularly exchanging their currencies, this can rack up quite a bit of fees in a fairly short amount of time.

With a global currency, such as a cryptocurrency, exchanges would be obsolete. Because the entire globe would operate with the same currency, the exchanges and fees related to exchanges would be unnecessary. People would have the option to use the cryptocurrency instead of a traditional currency, and this alternative would save them a significant amount of money. This is a positive change for both industries and consumers alike.

Disrupting a Stagnant Industry

As you may be able to tell by looking at the past few generations, the financial industry is one that has not changed much in a long period of time. While banks and other financial institutions have somewhat evolved and added new services and features for their clients, the industry as a whole has not seen much change. In general, it has always been the same in terms of client and bank relations.

The introduction of bitcoin, or any other cryptocurrency, particularly if it were to become a prominent currency, would entirely disrupt the current system. Banks themselves would be forced to change the way they do business, be more user-friendly and approachable for their clients, and offer better and more affordable services or they would eventually be driven out by cryptocurrencies. This means that the very structure by which our society is built on, currency, would be shaken and it would have the opportunity to change in favor of society, rather than to continue changing in favor of the banks.

Introducing New Technologies

In addition to all of the ways society itself would change, bitcoin and its underlying technology block chain have the power to help us introduce incredible new futuristic technologies into our society. Although it may seem like this new currency would essentially just swap out our traditional currency and step into its footsteps, this isn't entirely true. While it would fulfill all of the roles of traditional currency, it would also provide us with the opportunity to use and experience money in a way that we have never been able to before.

For example, we may be able to eventually drive cars that are equipped with payment systems within them that are hooked up to our unique cryptocurrency key. Then, whenever we park that car on a specific pad in parking lots it would be charged electronically and then the pad would be able to automatically charge our account for whatever the fee of "refueling" was. Or, fridges may be able to recognize when to order groceries and automatically order them for us, then take the cost off of our account automatically. We may even have the opportunity to have a smart house where we simply input what we need or want into a machine and it automatically orders it at a predetermined date and charges our account without us ever having to be involved beyond simply telling the machine that we wanted or needed something.

Based on the technology that bitcoin was built on, as well as bitcoin itself, there is an infinite number of potential new technologies that could be introduced that would revolutionize the way we live our lives. We truly could be living in a futuristic sci-fi inspired world sometime in the next few decades.

The future of our society may not even include bitcoin to begin with, but the fact that we are rapidly developing technologies to bring us into a futuristic world remains unchanged. Furthermore, as developers continue researching bitcoin and other cryptocurrencies, the idea of living in this futuristic world is no longer as far off as we once thought. If you recall the amount of change we have experienced since the invention of and introduction of computers back in the mid-1950s, then you can see that technology advances rapidly. Without a doubt, technology is going to continue advancing and in one way or another it may be able to advance in such a way that we could reap all of the benefits that have been outlined within this chapter. While it may seem like a dream to some, it is something that is not far off from our eventual reality.

Conclusion

Thank you for reading *Bitcoin: A Deep Dive into Bitcoin in the Age of Cryptocurrency*.

I hope that this book was able to provide you with deeper insight into the world of cryptocurrency and all that it has to offer us. With the help of cryptocurrency, we may eventually live in an incredible futuristic-themed world sooner than we originally anticipated. Furthermore, the invention of bitcoin has lead us to a greater understanding of the theory of cryptocurrency itself, how it could alter our society, and what is required in order to make a cryptocurrency that would be viable and truly usable.

The next step is to continue watching as bitcoin develops. Over the next few years it is likely that many advancements will be made. There is also the potential that the development of this technology could alter and take a route that we cannot presently predict. The future is as volatile as the bitcoin market, so knowing exactly where bitcoin and other cryptocurrencies will end up is highly unknown. One thing is for sure, however.

Cryptocurrencies are a highly admired theory and they are here to stay. Whether we like it or not, the reality of a digital currency is upon us and it is going to continue to be developed until it reaches a stage where it is either completely worthless to us and fades out, or where it becomes a prominent currency that people are able to use on a day to day basis. Naturally, we hope for the latter.

Finally, if you enjoyed this book and felt that it gave you value, I ask that you please take the time to review it on Amazon Kindle. Your honest feedback would be greatly appreciated.

Thank you.

Made in the USA
San Bernardino, CA
19 February 2019